2-at-a-time SOCKS

The Secret of Knitting Two at Once on One Circular Needle

Melissa Morgan-Oakes

Storey Publishing

The mission of Storey Publishing is to serve our customers by publishing practical information that encourages personal independence in harmony with the environment.

edited by: Gwen Steege and Erin Holman
art direction: Cynthia N. McFarland
cover design: Alethea Morrison and Leslie Anne Charles, LAC Design
book design and production: Leslie Anne Charles, LAC Design

photography: Kevin Kennefick
photo styling: Gladys Montgomery
illustrations: Alison Kolesar
charts: Lindsay Janeczek

cover sock: "Emily's Socks" (pages 104–109), knit by Kathleen M. Case
Knit in Valley Yarns Franklin (Kangaroo Dyer), WEBS, color Cancun
indexed by: Christine R. Lindemer, Boston Road Communications

© 2007 by Melissa Morgan-Oakes

Printed in Malaysia by Dai Nippon Printing

10 9 8 7

Library of Congress Cataloging-in-Publication Data

Morgan-Oakes, Melissa.
    2-at-a-time socks / Melissa Morgan-Oakes.
        p. cm.
    Includes index.
    ISBN 978-1-58017-691-0 (hardcover with concealed wire-o : alk. paper)
    1. Knitting—Patterns. 2. Socks. I. Title. II. Title: Two at a time socks.
TT825.M666 2008
746.43'2041—dc22

                                                                                    200703221

FOR NUMBER ONE,

and for his mother, G.W., who started it all.

TABLE OF CONTENTS

The
SECRET
Revealed

WHY TWO SOCKS AT ONCE? WELL, WHY NOT? Think about it. Two socks started and finished at the same time. They're still portable, still fun, but no "second-sock syndrome." For those who don't know about this knitting curse, it's what happens when a knitter completes the first sock and thinks "Oh, no. Now I have to make another one . . ." Often the finished sock and the yarn for its ne'er-to-be-knit pal get stuffed in a bag, never again to see the light of day. I've been whipping out socks two at a time for a few years now. And trust me, the rewards are great: All my socks are the same length. When I'm done with one sock, I am done with both. This may not be the method for everyone, but I think it's an excellent one for most people. Although never confronted with second-sock syndrome myself, I have seen its cruel effects on many a knitter; those victims deserve this technique.

While the concept is not by any means my own, I did develop my method independently of any outside source. It was not until the time came to write a book that I researched various sock-knitting techniques and found a bit more about how other folks are creating two socks at one time. My technique is different from others. It's not necessarily better, and I certainly don't think worse, but it is different. This book is not *just* about knitting two socks at once. It's about beautiful, funky, fun, creative, whimsical, and sophisticated socks. A knitter doesn't necessarily need to learn the technique in order to knit these socks; you can adapt these patterns to your personal sock-knitting style and still enjoy them. Are you a die-hard double pointer? That's okay. Addicted to other circular sock techniques? That's fine. With a little conversion, the patterns will work for you, too. But best of all, once you've mastered this technique, you can easily apply it to any of your favorite sock patterns.

Knitting did not come easily to me. One very beloved grandmother had taught me to crochet, but all my other relatives were knitters and wanted to teach me how to knit. Over a weekend visit, one grandmother would get me started, and I'd roll along nicely. The following weekend a different relative, perhaps a great-aunt would be knitting, and I'd ask if I could, too. Out would come needles and yarn, and I'd proudly demonstrate what I'd learned at Grandma's house. "What are you doing?" I'd hear. "I am knitting!" I'd reply, with the proud naivety of youth. "Well, you're not doing it right. Do it this way." Confused, I would comply, but my self-esteem suffered at my apparent lack of ability, and I tossed knitting out the window. Now I get it. Knitting crosses cultures. It changes shape along the way, and we've given names to its many forms: Continental. Combination. English. Eastern. Western. Crossed. Uncrossed. Knitters from very different cultural backgrounds were each trying to teach me how to knit *their* way.

While I was visiting my mother one day, her friend Stacia spied me knitting. She ripped my work out of my hands and told me I was doing it all wrong. I watched, stunned, as her fingers flew. I was trying to knit "the American way," and I needed to do it "the right way, the Polish way." Suddenly things seemed easier — in a matter of minutes I was knitting madly, purling joyfully, and having a total ball. I was a Knitter.

I began to knit constantly. Piles of baby sweaters appeared, even though no one was pregnant or planning to be. On weekends, my husband and I hiked, and that often meant long car rides to find new mountains. I created my first lace on a car trip. My first Fair Isle started the same way. It makes sense, then, that I turned my first heel in the car. Instantly hooked on the concept of socks, I took them everywhere. Portable. Fun. Adaptable. You can try anything with a sock; it's like a giant swatch.

A few weeks after I finished that first sock, I found WEBS. Although it feels like miles of fiber-filled space, WEBS is much more than a store: It's a community of knitters. Most important for me, it's become a place to teach and learn to grow as a knitting designer, and to help knitters of all backgrounds. WEBS is where I first taught knitting and the place that gave me a shot as a pattern designer and believed in me when I said, "I think I want to write a book about socks."

So here it is, a little book about socks and the method of knitting them that knitting friends have come to call "Melissa's Way." Within these pages, you'll find a technique that's probably new to you and a mix of sock patterns that I hope will inspire you. I've tried to include a lot of sizes and styles and a wide range of yarns, most

of which are machine washable and dryable. I have nothing against hand-washing socks and fully support the knitter's right to substitute any yarn you desire (as long as you get gauge), but I've learned from experience that socks sometimes get into places they don't belong (lost in a pant leg, for example) and disaster can result. So I rely heavily on machine-washable yarns for my own socks, and that bias is reflected in the book.

What I hope you'll most take away from this book is a spirit of adventure and play. Knitting should not be about deadlines, obsessive detail, or any form of stress. Few of us are making socks to keep our families from freezing their toes, so we can just have fun with our knitting. Knitting should be about liberation, freedom, expression, and joy. This is not to say that it's always easy or that new skills come without some effort. But the gain should outweigh the pain. The best cooks play with their food, the best fine artists play with their paints, and the best knitters play with their yarn — the only limits are the ones you place on yourself. Now grab a 40-inch long circular needle, and let's make socks!

2-at-a-time TECHNIQUE

SOCKS
are not difficult to knit,

though they can seem that way to the uninitiated. Actually, their construction requires only basic knitting skills.

The first thing any potential sock knitter should understand is the structure and anatomy of socks. Socks can be knit from the toe up, from the top down, or even sideways. There are at least five ways to create a turned heel in a top-down sock, and more than 10 toe treatments. In spite of these variations, the anatomy of a sock changes very little from one method of construction to another.

I will focus on a top-down sock method with a round heel and a reinforced heel flap. You begin top-down socks with a top *cuff*, usually worked in a narrow rib, though possibly in a fancy stitch that may create a ruffle or other attractive edging. Knit the *leg* next, then, on half the stitches, the *heel flap*, after which you work the *heel turn*. The stitches you don't use in creating the heel will become the *instep*, which, in the finished sock, will cover the top of the foot. After the heel turn come the *gusset* stitches, which you pick up from the heel flap, then decrease away, leaving a triangle of fabric. Next, you knit the *foot* and finally the *toe*. (For photo of sock anatomy, see next page.)

Sock Anatomy

If you understand the language and anatomy of socks, you'll be able to really see the part of the sock you are knitting, and reading patterns will become much simpler. It's also often helpful to think of sock patterns in terms of percentages: If the total number of cast-on stitches for each sock is 100%, instep and heel stitches are each generally 50%. When you add gussets and then decrease them away, you usually return the number of stitches to the original cast-on 100%, with 50% of the stitches in the instep (again) and 50% in the sole of the foot. Using this information, you can adapt any sock pattern to your particular style and the particular feet you're knitting for.

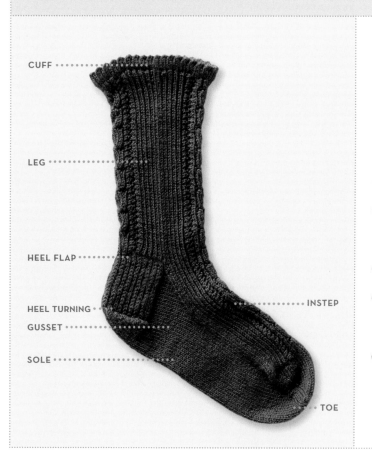

CUFF

LEG

HEEL FLAP

HEEL TURNING

GUSSET

SOLE

INSTEP

TOE

For most new sock knitters, confusion is born out of a lack of understanding of basic sock anatomy and the language used to describe it.

Knitting a Sample Sock

For the sake of practice, I'll demonstrate the 2-at-a-time method with these sample toddler socks. When completed, they should fit a two-to-three-year-old child, and they can make great gifts: Little kids don't mind if their socks are not perfect! You'll need one US 4 (3.5 mm), 40″ (100 cm) circular needle. I used Skacel's Addi Turbo, but any circular needle of this length will work. Stainless steel needles are especially good for circular techniques; the slippery metal allows stitches to move freely along the needle shaft, even when they are very tight — and you'll want to keep stitches tight at the end of each needle to prevent laddering (see The Lowdown on Laddering, page 17).

To make the transitions between socks easy to see, I suggest using two different colors of yarn for the sample socks. For these small socks, you should not need more than 60 yards each of two different colors of any worsted-weight yarn; I used Valley Yarns Superwash for the sample socks. The gauge is six stitches per inch, although at this point gauge is not a critical issue. (That may be the only time I *ever* say those words — gauge is actually always critical in garment construction. For more on gauge, see page 134.) Choose yarn colors similar to those shown in the photos — it will be easier for you to follow along.

You'll also need a stitch marker. I like to use Clover's locking stitch markers because I can attach them to my work to mark the beginning of rounds without damaging the yarn.

US 4 (3.5mm),
40″ CIRCULAR NEEDLE   TWO DIFFERENT-COLORED YARNS   STITCH MARKERS

Casting On

Step 1...With color A, use the long-tail method (see page 133) to cast 32 stitches onto your long circular needle. With color B, cast on 32 stitches.

sock B at needle tip

sock B

sock A

casting on

Step 2...Push both sets of newly cast-on stitches all the way down the cable to the other end of the needle (in your left hand). The yarn tails and working yarns should be away from the nearest working tip of the needle.

sock A at needle tip

pushing to left-hand end

Dividing and Joining Sock A

Step 3...You are now ready to divide the first set of cast-on stitches of sock A so that half of the stitches are on a working needle and half are on the cable, with a loop of cable between them. Slide the stitches back a bit until they are all on the cable. Starting at the first cast-on stitch, count back 16 stitches. Carefully separate the stitches and tug the cable through the opening, dividing the stitches exactly in half. (I use the point of my free needle to

2-at-a-time TIP

Ignorance Is Bliss
While you are working on Sock A, you should completely ignore the Sock B cast-on stitches.

elp pull the cable through.) Pull the cable through until it forms a
oop about 3″ (7.5 cm) long between the two sets of 16 stitches of
ock A. You have divided sock A stitches in half.

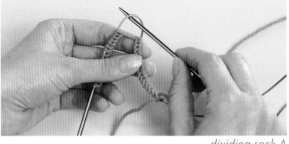

dividing sock A

tep 4… You now join the first and last stitches of sock A so you can
nit in the round, creating the cuff of your sock. Slide the half of the
titches that begins with the first cast-on stitch toward the nearest
eedle point.

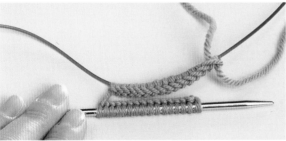

sliding first cast-on to tip

tep 5…Being careful not to twist your stitches, bring the work-
ig yarn of sock A up between the needles, letting the cast-on tail
ang down. Using the empty needle in your right hand, join the front
titches (the ones on the left-hand needle) to the back stitches (the
nes on the cable) with your working yarn by knitting into the first
ast-on stitch.

joining sock A

Step 6... Attach a locking stitch marker or scrap of contrasting color yarn to your work one stitch over from your join. Work these 16 stitches in a K1, P1 rib. This marks the beginning of the first round of sock A.

attaching stitch marker

Step 7... Rotate your work counterclockwise so that you can work the next 16 stitches of sock A (instep stitches). Push the unknit (cast on) stitches of sock A onto the needle in your left hand, and pull the right-hand needle through so that a few inches of cable are visible. Now, work the remaining 16 stitches of sock A in K1, P1 rib.

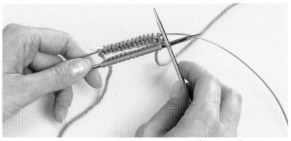

working sock A instep

Dividing and Joining Sock B

You've made it through the first round of sock A and are ready to join sock B so that it too can be worked in the round. Be careful not to lose the loop that separates the two groups of stitches of sock A. Allow sock A to rest close to the working stitches of sock B, but not close enough that you might confuse your socks.

Step 8… Allow sock A to remain under your right hand, with a loop of cable clearly visible. Slide the stitches of sock B down toward the needle in your left hand. The first cast-on stitch of sock B should be nearest the needle point.

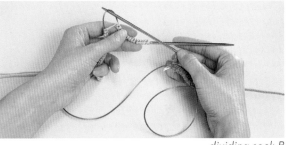

dividing sock B

Step 9… Divide the stitches into two sets of 16, placing half on the front needle and half on the cable. Be certain that the cast-on stitches of sock B are not twisted, and bring the working yarn of sock B up between the needles, allowing the cast-on tail to hang down. Using the working yarn of sock B, knit into the first cast-on stitch and work across these 16 stitches in K1, P1 rib (instep stitches).

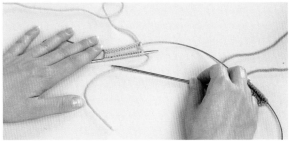

beginning sock B instep stitches

2-at-a-time **TIP**

The Lowdown on Laddering

"Ladders" are the open lines of stitches resembling the rungs of a ladder that can develop where needles come together. Be sure to pull tightly on your working yarn before and after needle changes to keep stitches good and tight. This will help prevent laddering!

Step 10... Working in the round, move on to the other side of sock B. Work in K1, P1 rib across the remainder of sock B stitches. You've finished one round on each sock, and are back at the center between the two socks.

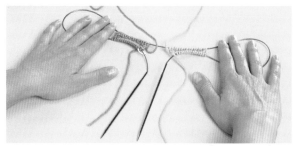

completing round one

Working the Cuffs and Legs

Step 11... Continue working first sock A and then sock B in K1, P1 rib until the piece measures 1½" (3.75 cm) from the cast-on edge.

completing cuffs

Step 12... Knit every round (stockinette stitch) until the socks measure 4½" (11.25 cm) from cast-on edge. End your leg-building at the end of a round.

completing leg

Working the Heel Flaps

My favorite heel flap is a simple one that creates a reinforced heel by using slipped stitches and knit stitches alternately on the right side of the work. *Note:* Work heel flaps on half of the total number of cast-on stitches.

Step 13... With the right side facing, begin working the heel flap of sock A. Slip the first stitch as if to purl, knit the next stitch. Continue across these 16 stitches in a slip 1, K1 pattern, ending with K1.

working row 1 of heel flap A

Step 14... Turn your work, slip the first stitch, and purl to the end of the row. You are now back in the center, between socks A and B.

completing row 2 of heel flap A

Step 15... Work the first heel-flap row of sock B. Note that this is a wrong-side row: Slip the first stitch, then purl to the end of the row. Turn your work.

An Exception to Every Rule

When do I knit socks one at a time? In those rare cases when I'm doing complex color work that requires more than two strands at a time or for large areas where tangling yarn could drive me to distraction, I work any main-color sections on both socks with one long circular needle. For the complicated bit, I move one sock to a short piece of scrap yarn or to double-pointed needles and then complete the colorwork separately on both socks. Once that's done, I return them both to one long circular for finishing together.

Step 16… Slip the first stitch of the right side of heel flap B, knit the next stitch. Continue across these 16 stitches as above, alternating a slip stitch and a knit stitch, ending with K1.

purl row of heel flap B

Step 17… Continue on heel flap A, working in the established slip 1, K1 pattern across the row, turn your work, slip the first stitch, and purl back across all stitches on heel flap A. Next, slip the first stitch of heel flap B, and purl across heel flap B. Work both heel flaps in turn in this way, alternating a slip 1, K1 row (right side) with a purl row (wrong side) on each sock until the heel flaps measure 1″ (2.5 cm). End having just worked a right-side row of heel flap B. Sock B will be a row shorter than sock A, but that's okay.

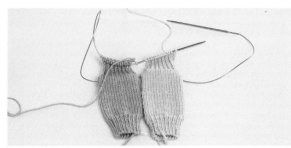

completing heel flaps

Turning the Heels

You will turn the heels using a short-row technique: Knit partway across the row, then turn your work and work partway back again. Continue in this way, working progressively more stitches across each row until you've worked all the stitches — and you've turned the heel. For the 2-at-a-time method, you work each heel turn separately, beginning with heel flap A. (See page 132 for explanations of the ssk [slip, slip, knit] and the P2tog [purl two together] decreases.)

Step 18... On heel flap A, K10, ssk, K1, turn. (This completes a right-side row.)

Step 19... Slip the first stitch, P5, P2tog, P1, turn. (This is a wrong-side row.) Take a moment to look at your work with the right side facing you. To your left, you have a series of eight just-worked stitches. If you look across these stitches, you'll see a small gap between stitches 8 and 9; you will close this gap as you create the short rows.

2-at-a-time TIP

Daring to Be Different
Not all sock patterns result in your ending on a wrong-side row. Each heel flap can be different, based on the number of stitches involved.

short-row gap

Step 20... Slip 1, K6 (you are now at one stitch before the gap, shown above), ssk (this closes the gap), K1, turn.

closing the gap

Step 21... Slip 1, P7 (you are now one stitch before the gap), P2tog (this closes the gap), P1, turn.

Step 22... Continue working short rows until all stitches have been worked and you have 10 stitches for the heel flap of sock A. You'll end with a wrong-side row.

completing sock A heel turn

Step 23... Move to sock B, slip the first stitch of the heel flap, and purl to the end of the row. Turn, and follow short-row heel-turn directions for sock A. You'll end having just worked a wrong-side row.

completing sock B heel turn

Step 24... With the right side of your work facing you, use the needle that is in your right hand to knit across the heel stitches of sock B, placing a marker between the fifth and sixth stitches of the heel. This marker (at the middle of the heel of sock B) denotes the new beginning of your rounds. You do not need to place a marker on sock A; the one on sock B will serve as the starting point for both of them.

placing marker at center of sock B

Picking Up Gusset Stitches

Simply put, gussets are extra material that make space and improve it. A handknitted tube sock will cover the foot, but it won't ever be as comfortable as a sock with a gusset, which accommodates the angle of the human foot. So now that you've created a turned heel, you need to make a gusset that will comfortably fit your heel. To accomplish this, you'll pick up stitches along both sides of the heel flaps and then decrease some of them away to create a triangular section of fabric (the gusset).

Step 25... Pick up and knit eight stitches along the left side of the heel flap of sock B. Note the clean line of ready-to-pick-up stitches you created by slipping a stitch at the beginning of every row while you worked the heel flap.

picking up along sock B heel flap

Step 26... To avoid a gap at the join between the gusset and instep, pick up and knit a ninth stitch between the heel and instep.

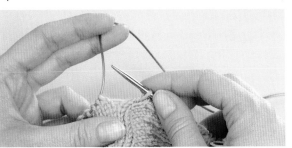

picking up extra stitch at instep

2-at-a-time TIP

Kinked Cables

No one likes a kinky cable. Avoid kinks by easing the cable through without creasing it. Kinks created in Addi Turbo needles are permanent. The cables of these needles are made of a steel wire coated with flexible nylon; once bent, the internal wire stays bent. I still love them!

Step 27... Move to sock A, work across the heel stitches. (Don't worry about the stitches on the right side of sock A heel flap yet; you will pick up these in Step 30.) Pick up and knit eight stitches along the left side of the heel flap of sock A, then pick up a stitch between the heel and instep.

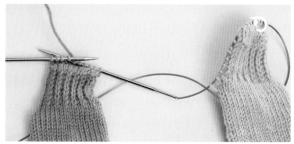

working across sock A heel stitches

Step 28... Working in the round once again, move to the instep stitches. Adjust your cables as shown, and work across the insteps of both socks.

working both insteps

Step 29... Pick up and knit one stitch between the sock B instep and heel flap, then pick up and knit eight gusset stitches on the right side of heel flap B. Work across the heel stitches of sock B and down the left heel flap. (Adjust needles so that the cable loop separates the instep stitches of sock B from the newly picked up gusset stitches.)

picking up gusset stitches of sock A

2-at-a-time **TIP**

Keeping the Parts Straight

Your instep stitches should always be on one side of the cable, and the gusset and heel stitches should always be on the other.

Step 30... Pick up and knit a stitch between the sock A instep and heel flap, then pick up and knit eight stitches along the right side of the sock A heel flap. You've now picked up all heel flap stitches. Work all the way around to the marker on sock B. The instep stitches should be together on one side of the needle, and the heel flap and gusset stitches should be together on the other side.

Working the Gusset Decreases

Step 31... Knit to last three stitches of sock B, K2tog, K1. Move to sock A. K1, ssk, knit to last three stitches of sock A, K2tog, K1. Work across the instep stitches of socks A and B. On Sock B sole (gusset) stitches, K1, ssk, knit to marker. Your first round of gusset decreases is complete. (See photo below for location of decreases.) Continue across sole (gusset) stitches as you begin next round.

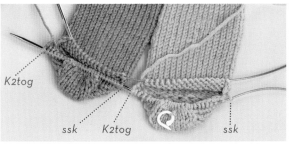

decrease round completed, next round begun

Step 32... Knit one round without decreasing, knitting all stitches on socks A and B until you are back to the marker on sock B. Next, repeat the gusset decrease round (Step 31).

2-at-a-time TIP

Extra Stitches?
Funny loops you don't remember inviting to the party? Be wary of inadvertently creating yarn overs! When starting a new section of stitches, always keep your working yarn between front and back, or needle and cable. Don't bring your yarn up over the needles from behind the back cable, or you will end up with more stitches than you counted on.

Keeping Your Yarns Straight

For most pairs of socks, you won't be knitting two socks in different colors, so it's important to identify which yarn belongs to which sock. When you switch socks, be sure to grab the correct yarn for the sock you're knitting: You'll know if you make a mistake here when sock A and sock B become joined together — perfect if your pogo stick needs socks, but not so handy for humans! If this happens, simply unknit the offending stitches as soon as you notice them, and then proceed with the right yarn.

Step 33... Continue working alternating decrease and even rounds (Steps 31 and 32) until 16 stitches remain on both the heel and instep sides of both socks A and B — 32 stitches total for each sock. You will be able to see the neat triangles on each side of your socks, created by the mirror-image ssk and K2tog decreases.

completing gusset decreases

Knitting the Foot

Step 34... Work in stockinette stitch on the remaining stitches (32 on each sock) until the sole of each sock from the back of the heel measures 4″ (10 cm).

completing the soles

Shaping the Toe

Your socks are nearly done! It's time to shape their toes. You will work toe decreases in the same manner as gusset decreases: To create a smooth appearance, use an ssk decrease on one side of the toe box and a K2tog decrease on the other.

Step 35...At this point, your "beginning-of-the-round" marker makes its final move: Attach it to the first sole stitch of sock B.

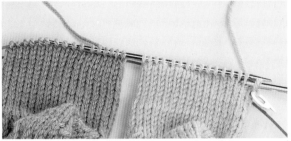

attaching marker for new round

Step 36...Work one more round on all stitches just to the marker (newly placed at the beginning of the sole of sock B). On sock B, K1, ssk, knit to the last three stitches of sock B, K2tog, K1. On sock A, K1, ssk, knit to the last three stitches of sock A, K2tog, K1.

Step 37...Continuing to work in the round, repeat these decreases on the instep side of both socks. This completes the first round of toe decreases.

Step 38...Work one round even, knitting all stitches.

Step 39... Alternate decrease and even rounds (Steps 36–38) three more times (eight rounds total). You should have eight stitches remaining on the sole and the instep of each section of both socks. Work three more decrease rounds, with no even rows between. You should now have two stitches remaining in each section of both socks, a total of four stitches on each sock.

completing toe decreases

2-at-a-time
TIP

Subduing Circulars
New circular needles often cause "laddering" (see page 17): The needles come neatly coiled in their packages, and they want to stay tightly wound, which can cause pulled, distorted stitches. Soaking them in very hot water for a minute or two can reduce this problem. I boil water in my microwave for three minutes, then hold just the cable — not the needles or the needle join — in the water for a minute or so to loosen the cables up a bit. I've even soaked them in the coffee of a certain fast-food franchise: If it's hot enough to start lawsuits, it's hot enough to soften my cable.

Many knitters seem to have heard at least one grafting horror story. In class, when I teach grafting (also known as Kitchener Stitch), I start with a couple of ground rules: First, everyone must forget everything bad or scary that they've ever heard about it. Kitchener Stitch is, after all, part of knitting, so it should not be frightening, intimidating, or threatening. Rather, it's a skill to learn and embrace. The second thing I tell students about Kitchener Stitch is that usually the best way to learn it is simply to do it. At first, it makes very little visual sense — it took me a long time to "get" what was happening when I was learning it.

When you first try Kitchener Stitch, find another knitter or a sympathetic spouse or friend to slowly read the directions to you as you take each step. (Trying to read about Kitchener and do it at the same time can be confounding.) It's helpful to remember that stitches are worked in groups of two, and each stitch gets worked twice.

Grafting the Toe

Step 40... Note: Work Kitchener Stitch on each toe separately. To begin, cut the yarn, leaving a tail 10" (25.5 cm) long, and thread this tail onto a darning needle. Bring all the stitches to the tips of the circular needle, holding the needles parallel with the points facing to the right, and the cable on the left.

Step 41... Bring the darning needle through the first stitch on the front needle as if to purl, pulling the yarn through the stitch while leaving the stitch on the needle.

Front, purl

Step 42... Bring the yarn through the first stitch on the back needle as if to knit, leaving it on the needle.

Back, knit

Step 43…Work the first stitch on the front needle as if to knit, drawing the yarn through the stitch, then slide it off the knitting needle.

Front knit and off

Step 44…Work the next stitch on the first needle as if to purl, and leave it on the knitting needle (see photo for step 41).

Step 45…Work the first stitch on the back needle as if to purl, then slide it off the knitting needle.

Back purl and off

Step 46…Work the next stitch on the back needle as if to knit, and leave it on the knitting needle.

Repeat Steps 43-46 until one stitch remains on each needle. Finish by working the front stitch as if to knit, and sliding it off the needle, then working the back stitch as if to purl, and sliding it off the knitting needle. To finish, simply draw the tail to the inside and weave it in for a few stitches.

Ahhh, Sweet Success!

You've just joined the ranks of knitters who are no longer victims of second-sock syndrome. You can now move forward, confident in your new skill, safe from the legions of single socks lying in bags and hidden in stash bins everywhere. With a very few exceptions, this is the only way I knit socks. The socks are still portable, still adorable, and still fun to knit. Now, they're also always the same length, done in one fell swoop, and *really* fun to knit. Two socks, at once. What could be better?

The 17 knitting patterns that follow range in skill level from beginner to advanced and use a variety of yarn weights. Some feature cables, Fair Isle, and lots of stitch combinations, all easily knitted two at a time on one circular needle.

I offer each pattern in three sizes, including some designed for the littlest feet. Obviously, making socks that *fit* is important, so I tell you the finished foot circumferences for each size. I also include directions for adapting the length of each pattern for your specific needs, so you can get a custom fit every time. Patterns ultimately are guidelines, and nothing is written in stone. Enjoy!

2-at-a-time PATTERNS

Berry Season

As the growing season moves along, I often end up with half a quart of one berry and a quart of another. Rather than waste anything, I throw it into a pie shell or mash it up and turn it into mixed-berry jam. Knit in bright jewel tones, these socks make me think of in-season berries, all that gleaming fresh color begging for a taste. They knit up quickly, with a little bit of patterning for texture. Wear them while you're picking all that fruit!

YARN	Cherry Tree Hill Superwash Merino Mini, 100% merino wool, sport weight, 4 oz (113 g)/280 yds (256 m). Yarn band gauge: 5.5 stitches = 1″ (2.5 cm) in Stockinette Stitch on US 5 (3.75 mm) needles Winterberry: 1 skein
GAUGE	6 stitches and 7 rows = 1″ (2.5 cm) in Stockinette Stitch
NEEDLE	US 4 (3.25 mm) 40″ (100 cm) long circular, *or size needed to obtain correct gauge*
NOTIONS	Stitch markers, tape measure, darning needle
SIZES	**M** Women's Medium **LS** Women's Large/Men's Small **M** Men's Medium

FINISHED FOOT CIRCUMFERENCE

M 8″ (20.25 cm)
LS 9¼″ (23.5 cm)
M 10″ (25.5 cm)

Pattern Stitches

GARTER STITCH
ROUND 1 Knit.
ROUND 2 Purl.
Repeat these two rounds.

STOCKINETTE STITCH
Knit every round.

RIBBING
K2, P2.

BERRY SEASON STITCH
ROUND 1 * K2, slip 2 wyib as if to purl; repeat from * to end of round.
ROUND 2 K2, P2 to end of round.
ROUND 3 * Slip 2 wyib as if to purl, K2; repeat from * to end of round.
ROUND 4 P2, K2 to end of round.

Knitting the Legs

Set Up For each sock, cast on   **M** 48 sts   **L S** 56 sts   **M** 60 sts

Note If desired, attach locking stitch marker or scrap of contrasting color yarn to your work one stitch over from your join on sock A to mark the beginning of your work.

Rounds 1–4 Work in Garter Stitch.

Rounds 5–10 Work in Stockinette Stitch.

Next Rounds K2, P2 for 1″ (2.5 cm).

Next Rounds Work Berry Season Stitch (see page 32) until leg measurement from cast-on edge is   **M** 4″ (10 cm)   **L S** 4¼″ (10.75 cm)   **M** 4½″ (11.5 cm)

Note End ready to begin sock A heel. Remove any markers used to denote beginning of round, and reserve for later.

Working the Heel Flaps

Note Work the heel flaps for both socks in rows at the same time on   **M** 24 sts   **L S** 28 sts   **M** 30 sts

Row 1 * Slip 1 stitch with yarn in back, K1; repeat from * to end of row.

Row 2 Slip the first stitch; purl to end of row. (Note that the first heel flap row for sock B is Row 2.)

Next Rows Repeat Rows 1 and 2   **M** 12 more times   **L S** 13 more times   **M** 14 more times

End having just worked Row 2.

The heel flaps now measure about   **M** 2″ (5 cm)   **L S** 2¼″ (5.75 cm)   **M** 2½″ (6.25 cm)

Turning the Heels

Note Turn the heel on each sock separately, working in rows and beginning with sock A.

Row 1

- Knit   **M** 14 sts   **L S** 16 sts   **M** 17 sts

- Ssk, K1, turn.

Row 2 Slip1, P5, P2tog, P1, turn.

Row 3 Slip1, knit to one stitch before gap, ssk to close gap, K1, turn.

Row 4 Slip1, purl to one stitch before gap, P2tog to close gap, P1, turn.

Next Rows Repeat Rows 3 and 4 until all stitches have been worked.

Sock A heel now has   **M** 14 sts   **LS** 16 sts   **M** 17 sts

Follow directions above to turn sock B heel.

Picking Up Stitches for Gussets

Note Begin by picking up stitches on left side of sock B heel.

Pick-Up Round

- Knit across sock B heel. Place a marker at the center of sock B heel. This represents the new beginning of rounds. With right side facing and working along the left side of sock B heel, pick up and knit   **M** 13 sts   **LS** 14 sts   **M** 15 sts

- Move to sock A, and knit across the heel stitches.

- Along left side of sock A heel, pick up and knit   **M** 13 sts   **LS** 14 sts   **M** 15 sts

- Work Berry Season Stitch Pattern as established across sock A and B instep stitches.

- Along right side of sock B heel, pick up and knit   **M** 13 sts   **LS** 14 sts   **M** 15 sts

- Knit across heel stitches to marker, slide marker, work the remainder of sock B heel. Along right side of sock A heel, pick up and knit   **M** 13 sts   **LS** 14 sts   **M** 15 sts

- Continue as established to the marker at the center of sock B heel.

Working the Gusset Decreases

Round 1

- On sock B heel, work to last 3 stitches, K2tog, K1.
- On sock A heel, K1, ssk, knit to last 3 stitches, K2tog, K1.

- Work instep stitches as established on both socks. (Don't decrease on the instep stitches.)
- On sock B heel, K1, ssk, knit to marker. You have completed the first round of gusset decreases.

Round 2 Work even on all stitches as established.

Next Rounds Repeat Rounds 1 and 2 until each sock contains
   M 48 sts   **LS** 56 sts   **M** 60 sts

Working the Sock Feet

Continue on these stitches as established, working no further decreases, until the measurement from the back of the heel is

   M 7¼"   **LS** 8"   **M** 9"
     (18.5 cm)   (20.25 cm)   (22.75 cm)

or 2" (5 cm) less than the length of the foot of the intended wearer.

Decreasing for the Toes

Set Up Work one more round, ending at the beginning of sock B sole. Move the marker from the center of sock B sole to the beginning of sock B sole, to mark the new beginning of rounds.

Round 1

- On sock B sole, K1, ssk, knit to last 3 stitches, K2tog, K1.
- On sock A sole, K1, ssk, knit to last 3 stitches on sole, K2tog, K1.
- On sock A instep, K1, ssk, knit to last 3 stitches on instep, K2tog, K1.
- On sock B instep, K1, ssk, knit to last 3 stitches on instep, K2tog, K1.

Round 2 Knit all stitches.

Next Rounds Repeat Rounds 1 and 2   **M** 5 more times   **LS** 6 more times   **M** 7 more times

Next Rounds Repeat Round 1   **M** 4 more times   **LS** 5 more times   **M** 5 more times

Each sock now has 8 stitches total: 4 instep and 4 sole stitches.

Follow the Kitchener Stitch instructions on pages 28–29 to graft the toes closed.

Finishing

Weave in any loose ends. Block both socks, following the instructions on page 134.

BERRY SEASON STITCH PATTERN

		•	•	4
		V•	V•	3
•	•			2
V•	V•			1
4	3	2	1	

key

☐ Knit

• Purl

V Slip as if to purl

Spice

A little colorwork can go a long way. This fun-to-knit color pattern livens up a fairly simple sock, and the contrasting heel and toe throw in even more entertainment value. A nicely twisted yarn is great for working in color; its excellent stitch definition enhances the work you've put in.

YARN	Louet Gems Merino Superfine, 100% merino, fingering weight, 1.75 oz (50 g)/185 yds (169 m). Yarn band gauge: 6.5–7.5 stitches = 1" (2.5 cm) in Stockinette Stitch on US 2–3 (2.75–3.25 mm) needles MC = ginger 02: 2 skeins CA = champagne 01: 1 skein CB = eggplant 42: 1 skein CC = terra cotta 47: 1 skein
GAUGE	9 stitches and 10 rows = 1" (2.5 cm) in Stockinette Stitch
NEEDLE	US 2 (2.75 cm) 40" (100 cm) circular, or *size needed to obtain correct gauge*
NOTIONS	Stitch markers, tape measure, darning needle
SIZES	S Women's Small M Women's Medium L Women's Large
FINISHED FOOT CIRCUMFERENCE	S 8" (20.25 cm) M 9" (22.75 cm) L 10" (25.5 cm)

Pattern Stitches

RIBBING
K2, P2.

STOCKINETTE STITCH
Knit every round.

Knitting the Legs

Set Up For each sock, using MC cast on **S** 72 sts **M** 80 sts **L** 88 sts

Note If desired, attach locking stitch marker or scrap of contrasting color yarn to your work one stitch over from your join on sock A to mark the beginning of your work.

Rounds 1–7 Work in K2, P2 ribbing for ¾" (2 cm).

Rounds 8–19 Work Spice Socks Color Chart (see page 43).

S 9	**M** 10	**L** 11
times per round	times per round	times per round

Next Rounds In MC, work in K2, P2, ribbing, until leg measurement from cast-on edge is

S 6"	**M** 6½"	**L** 7"
(15.25 cm)	(16.5 cm)	(17.75 cm)

Note End ready to begin sock A heel. Remove any markers used to denote beginning of round, and reserve for later.

Working the Heel Flaps

Note In CA, work the heel flaps for both socks in rows at the same time on **S** 36 sts **M** 40 sts **L** 44 sts

Row 1 *Slip 1 stitch with yarn in back, K1; repeat from * to end of row.

Row 2 Slip the first stitch; purl to the end of row. (Note that the first heel flap row for sock B is Row 2.)

Next Rows Repeat Rows 1 and 2

S 17	**M** 19	**L** 21
more times	more times	more times

End having just worked Row 2.

The heel flaps now measure about

S 2"	**M** 2¼"	**L** 2½"
(5 cm)	(5.75 cm)	(6.25 cm)

Turning the Heels

Note Turn the heel on each sock separately, beginning with sock A.

Row 1

- Knit across first **S** 20 sts **M** 22 sts **L** 24 sts

- Ssk, K1, turn.

Row 2 Slip 1, P5, P2tog, P1, turn.

Row 3 Slip 1, knit to one stitch before gap, ssk to close gap, K1, turn.

Row 4 Slip 1, purl to one stitch before gap, P2tog to close gap, P1, turn.

Next Rows Repeat Rows 3 and 4 until all stitches have been worked.

Sock A heel now has   **S** 20 sts   **M** 22 sts   **L** 24 sts

Follow directions above to turn sock B heel.

Picking Up Stitches for Gussets

Note Begin by picking up stitches on left side of sock B heel.

Pick-Up Round

- In MC, knit across sock B heel. Place a marker at the center of sock B heel. This represents the new beginning of rounds. With right side facing, along the left side of sock B heel pick up and knit

    S 18 sts   **M** 20 sts   **L** 22 sts

- Move to sock A, and knit across the heel stitches.
- Along left side of sock A heel, pick up and knit

    S 18 sts   **M** 20 sts   **L** 22 sts

- Work K2, P2 ribbing as established across sock A and B instep stitches.
- Along right side of sock B heel, pick up and knit

    S 18 sts   **M** 20 sts   **L** 22 sts

- Knit across sock B heel stitches to marker, slip marker, work left side of sock B heel. Along right side of sock A heel, pick up and knit

    S 18 sts   **M** 20 sts   **L** 22 sts

- Continue as established to the marker at the center of sock B heel.

Working the Gusset Decreases

Round 1

- On sock B heel, work to last 3 stitches, K2tog, K1.
- On sock A heel, K1, ssk, knit to last 3 stitches, K2tog, K1.
- Knit instep stitches in K2, P2 ribbing on both socks. (Don't decrease on the instep stitches.)

- On sock B heel, K1, ssk, knit to marker. You have completed the first round of gusset decreases.

Round 2   Work even on all stitches.

Next Rounds   Repeat Rounds 1 and 2 until each sock contains   **S** 72 sts   **M** 80 sts   **L** 88 sts

Working the Sock Feet

Continue on these stitches as established, working no further decreases, until the measurement from the back of the heel is   **S** 6½"   **M** 7"   **L** 7¼"

        (16.5 cm)   (17.75 cm)   (18.5 cm)

or 1½" (3.75 cm) less than the length of the foot of the intended wearer.

Decreasing for the Toes

Set Up   Work one more round, ending at the beginning of sock B sole. Move the marker from the center of sock B sole to the beginning of the sock B sole, to mark the new beginning of rounds.

Round 1

- On sock B sole, K1, ssk, knit to last 3 stitches, K2tog, K1.
- On sock A sole, K1, ssk, knit to last 3 stitches, K2tog, K1.
- On sock A instep, K1, ssk, knit to last 3 stitches, K2tog, K1.
- On sock B instep, K1, ssk, knit to last 3 stitches, K2tog, K1.

Round 2   Knit all stitches.

Next Rounds   Change to CA. Work Rounds 1 and 2   **S** 7 more times   **M** 8 more times   **L** 9 more times

Next Rounds   Knit Round 1   **S** 6 more times   **M** 7 more times   **L** 8 more times

Each sock now has a total of 16 stitches: 8 instep and 8 sole stitches.

Follow the Kitchener Stitch instructions on pages 28–29 to graft the toes closed.

Finishing

Weave in any loose ends. Block both socks, following the instructions on page 134.

SPICE SOCKS COLOR CHART

									19
									18
									17
									16
									15
									14
									13
									12
									11
									10
									9
									8
									7
									6
									5
									4
									3
									2
									1
8	7	6	5	4	3	2	1		

key

■ MC = ginger 02
□ CA = champagne 01
■ CB = eggplant 42
■ CC = terra cotta 47

Be Mine

Once, a few years ago, I forgot about my wedding anniversary until the afternoon of the actual day. Racing home, I managed to produce a batch of M&M cookies and one mitten by the time my husband got back from work. For months I had planned to make Valentine socks for him. Once again, I forgot and found myself knitting socks as fast as I could. What I failed to consider is that men generally do not wear bright red socks with heart-shaped cables. But he wore them. More than once, even!

YARN   Lana Grossa Meilenweit 100, 80% wool/20% polyamid, fingering weight, 3½ oz (100 g)/462 yds (420 m). Yarn band gauge: 7 stitches and 10 rows = 1″ (2.5 cm) in Stockinette Stitch on US 1–2 (2.5–3 mm) needles.
Red 1326: 1 skein

GAUGE   7 stitches and 9 rows = 1″ in Stockinette Stitch

NEEDLE   US 2 (2.75 mm) 40″ (100 cm) long circular, *or size needed to obtain correct gauge*

NOTIONS   Stitch markers, tape measure, small cable needle, darning needle

SIZES   S Women's Small
M Women's Medium
L Women's Large

FINISHED FOOT CIRCUMFERENCE
S 8½″ (21.5 cm)
M 9″ (23 cm)
L 9½″ (24.25 cm)

Pattern Stitches

RIBBING
K1, P1.

STOCKINETTE STITCH
Knit every row.

Knitting the Legs

Set Up For each sock, cast on · S 60 sts · M 64 sts · L 68 sts

Note If desired, attach locking stitch marker or scrap of contrasting color yarn one stitch past join on sock A to mark the beginning of your work.

Work in K1, P1 ribbing for 1½" (3.75 cm).

Twice in each round, work the Be Mine Cable Pattern (see page 49).
S 30 sts · M 32 sts · L 34 sts

Complete 4 repeats of the Be Mine Cable Pattern, 64 rows total.

Leg measurement from cast-on edge is now about 8" (20.25 cm).

Note End ready to begin sock A heel. Remove any markers used to denote beginning of round, and reserve for later.

Working the Heel Flaps

Note Work the heel flaps for both socks in rows at the same time on
S 30 sts · M 32 sts · L 34 sts

Row 1 * Slip 1 stitch with yarn in back, K1; repeat from * to end of row.

Row 2 Slip the first stitch; purl to the end of row. (Note that the first heel flap row for sock B is Row 2.)

Next Rows Repeat Rows 1 and 2 · S 14 more times · M 15 more times · L 16 more times

End having just worked Row 2.

The heel flaps now measure about · S 2" (5 cm) · M 2¼" (5.75 cm) · L 2½" (6.25 cm)

Turning the Heels

Note Turn the heel on each sock separately, beginning with sock A.

Row 1

- Knit across first · S 17 sts · M 18 sts · L 18 sts
- Ssk, K1, turn.

Row 2 Slip 1, P5, P2tog, P1, turn.

Row 3 Slip 1, knit to one stitch before gap, ssk to close gap, K1, turn.

Row 4 Slip 1, purl to one stitch before gap, P2tog to close gap, P1, turn.

Next Rows Repeat Rows 3 and 4 until all stitches have been worked.

Sock A heel now has   **S** 17 sts   **M** 18 sts   **L** 19 sts

Follow directions above to turn sock B heel.

Picking Up Stitches for Gussets

Note Begin by picking up stitches on left side of sock B heel.

Pick-Up Round

- Knit across sock B heel. Place a marker at the center of sock B heel. This represents the new beginning of rounds. With right side facing, down the left side of sock B heel pick up and knit

     S 15 sts   **M** 16 sts   **L** 17 sts

- Move to sock A, and knit across the heel stitches.

- Along left side of sock A heel, pick up and knit

     S 15 sts   **M** 16 sts   **L** 17 sts

- Work Be Mine Cable Pattern as established across sock A and B instep stitches.

- Along right side of sock B heel, pick up and knit

     S 15 sts   **M** 16 sts   **L** 17 sts

- Knit across sock B heel stitches to marker, slip marker, work left side of sock B heel. Along right side of sock A heel, pick up and knit

     S 15 sts   **M** 16 sts   **L** 17 sts

- Continue as established to the marker at the center of sock B heel.

Working the Gusset Decreases

Round 1

- On sock B heel, work to last 3 stitches, K2tog, K1.

- On sock A heel, K1, ssk, knit to last 3 stitches, K2tog, K1.

- Continue knitting instep stitches in Be Mine Cable Pattern on both socks as established. (Don't decrease on the instep stitches.)

- On sock B heel, K1, ssk, knit to marker. You have completed the first round of gusset decreases.

Round 2 Work even on all stitches.

Next Rounds Repeat Rounds 1 and 2 until each sock contains

S	60 sts	M	64 sts	L	68 sts

Working the Sock Feet

Continue on these stitches as established, working no further decreases until the measurement from the back of the foot is

S	6½"	M	7"	L	7¼"
	(16.5 cm)		(17.75 cm)		(18.5 cm)

or 1½" (3.75 cm) less than the length of the foot of the intended wearer.

Decreasing for the Toes

Set Up Work one more round, ending at the beginning of sock B sole. Move the marker from the center of sock B sole to the beginning of sock B sole stitches, to mark the new beginning of rounds.

Round 1

- On sock B sole, K1, ssk, knit to last 3 stitches, K2tog, K1.
- On sock A sole, K1, ssk, knit to last 3 stitches, K2tog, K1.
- On sock A instep, K1, ssk, knit to last 3 stitches, K2tog, K1.
- On sock B instep, K1, ssk, knit to last 3 stitches, K2tog, K1.

Round 2

- Knit all stitches.

Knit Rounds 1 and 2

S	5 more times	M	6 more times	L	7 more times

Next Rounds Knit Round 1

S	5 more times	M	5 more times	L	5 more times

Each sock now has a total of 16 stitches: 8 instep and 8 sole stitches, .

Follow the Kitchener Stitch instructions on pages 28–29 to graft the toes closed.

Finishing

Weave in any loose ends. Block both socks, following the instructions on page 134.

BE MINE CABLE PATTERN

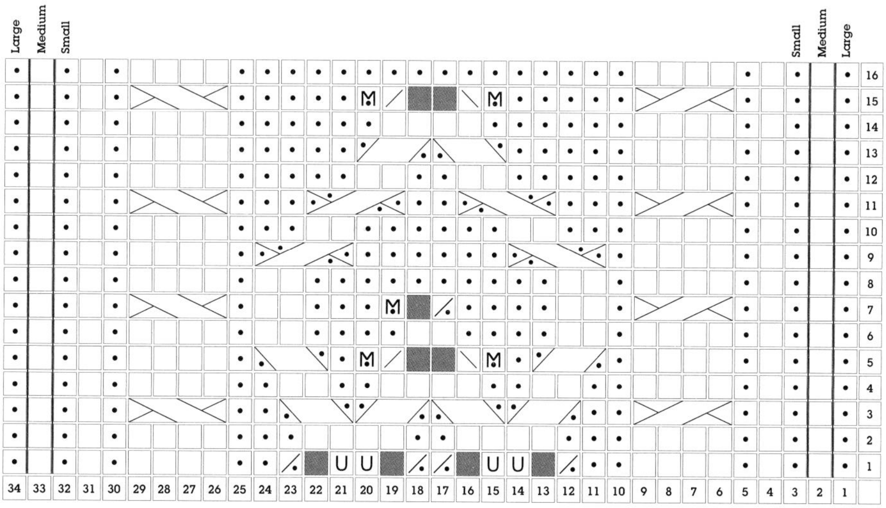

Row numbers (right to left along bottom): 34 33 32 31 30 29 28 27 26 25 24 23 22 21 20 19 18 17 16 15 14 13 12 11 10 9 8 7 6 5 4 3 2 1

Right-side labels (top and bottom): Large, Medium, Small

Row numbers (right edge, bottom to top): 1–16

key

☐	Knit
•	Purl
↘	Slip, slip, knit
╱	Knit 2 together
╱•	Purl 2 together
■	No stitch
U	Knit into the front and back
M	Purl into the front and back
⟍⟍	Slip 2 stitches to cable needle and hold in back, K2, K2 from cable needle
⟋⟍	Slip 2 stitches to cable needle and hold in front, K2, K2 from cable needle
⟋•	Slip 1 purl stitch to cable needle and hold in back, K2, P1 from cable needle
•⟍	Slip 2 knit stitches to cable needle and hold in front, P1, K2 from cable needle
•⟋•	Slip 2 purl stitches to cable needle and hold in back, K2, P2 from cable needle
•⟍•	Slip 2 stitches to cable needle and hold in front, P2, K2 from cable needle

Varsity

The colors of this sock make me think of fall and football games. Simple striping makes it visually appealing yet easy to knit, and stripes are a great way to play with color. For fun, customize the colorway to match the colors of a favorite school or team. Or just choose a few of your favorites!

YARN Valley Yarns Superwash, 100% extra fine merino wool, worsted weight, 1½ oz (50gm)/97yds (88 m). Yarn band gauge: 4.5 stitches = 1" (2.5 cm) in Stockinette Stitch on US 8 (5 mm) needles
CA = Rosewood 920: 1 skein
CB = Biscuit 419: 1 skein
CC = Forest 600: 1 skein
CD = Copper 861: 1 skein

GAUGE 6 sts and 9 rows = 1" (2.5 cm) in Stockinette Stitch

NEEDLE US 3 (3.25 mm) 40" (100 cm) circular, or size needed to obtain gauge

NOTIONS Stitch markers, tape measure, darning needle

SIZES
M Women's Medium
LS Women's Large/Men's Small
M Men's Medium

FINISHED FOOT CIRCUMFERENCE
M 8½" (21.5 cm)
LS 9¼" (23.5 cm)
M 10" (25.5 cm)

Pattern Stitches

RIBBING A
K1, P1.

RIBBING B
K3, P1.

STOCKINETTE STITCH
Knit every round.

VARSITY STRIPE SEQUENCE
ROUNDS 1 AND 2 Work in CB.
ROUNDS 3–6 Work in CC.
ROUNDS 7–12 Work in CD.
ROUNDS 13–14 Work in CB.
ROUNDS 15–18 Work in CA.

Knitting the Legs

Set Up In CA, for each sock cast on   M 52 sts   LS 56 sts   M 60 sts

Note If desired, attach locking stitch marker or scrap of contrasting color yarn to your work one stitch over from your join on sock A to mark the beginning of your work.

Work in K1, P1 ribbing for 2″ (5 cm).

In Varsity Stripe Sequence (see page 50), and ending at a color change, work in K3, P1 ribbing until leg measurement from cast-on edge is about

M 7″   LS 8″   M 9″
(17.75 cm)   (20.25 cm)   (22.75 cm)

Note End ready to begin sock A heel. Remove any markers used to denote beginning of round, and reserve for later.

Working the Heel Flaps

Note Using the next color in the Varsity Stripe Sequence, work the heel flaps for both socks in rows at the same time on

M 26 sts   LS 28 sts   M 30 sts

Row 1 * Slip 1 stitch with yarn in back, K1; repeat from * to end of row.

Row 2 Slip the first stitch; purl to the end of row. (Note that the first heel flap row for sock B is Row 2.)

Next Rows Repeat Rows 1 and 2

| M 12 more times | LS 13 more times | M 14 more times |

End having just worked Row 2.

The heel flaps now measure about

M 2″   LS 2¼″   M 2½″
(5 cm)   (5.75 cm)   (6.25 cm)

Turning the Heels

Note Turn the heel on each sock separately, working in rows, and beginning with sock A. (Continue in heel flap color.)

Row 1

- Knit across first   M 15 sts   LS 16 sts   M 17 sts

- Ssk, K1, turn.

Row 2 Slip 1, P5, P2tog, P1, turn.

Row 3 Slip 1, knit to one stitch before gap, ssk to close gap, K1, turn.

Row 4 Slip 1, purl to one stitch before gap, P2tog to close gap, P1, turn.

Next Rows Repeat Rows 3 and 4 until all stitches have been worked.

Sock A heel now has   **M** 15 sts   **L S** 16 sts   **M** 17 sts

Follow directions above to turn sock B heel.

Picking Up Stitches for Gussets

Note Begin by picking up stitches on left side of sock B heel.

Pick-Up Round

- Continuing in heel flap color, knit across sock B heel. Place a marker at the center of sock B heel. This represents the new beginning of rounds. With right side facing, along the left side of sock B heel pick up and knit   **M** 13 sts   **L S** 14 sts   **M** 15 sts

- Move to sock A, and knit across the heel stitches.

- Along left side of sock A heel, pick up and knit   **M** 13 sts   **L S** 14 sts   **M** 15 sts

- Work K3, P1 ribbing as established across sock A and B instep stitches.

- Along right side of sock B heel, pick up and knit   **M** 13 sts   **L S** 14 sts   **M** 15 sts

- Knit across sock B heel stitches to marker, slip marker, work left side of sock B heel. Along right side of sock A heel, pick up and knit   **M** 13 sts   **L S** 14sts   **M** 15 sts

- Continue as established to the marker at the center of sock B heel.

Working the Gusset Decreases

Note As you work gusset decreases and knit the sock foot, maintain Varsity Stripe Sequence as established.

Round 1

- On sock B heel, work to last 3 stitches, K2tog, K1.

- On sock A heel, K1, ssk, knit to last 3 stitches, K2tog, K1.

- Work instep stitches as established on both socks. (Don't decrease on the instep stitches.)
- On sock B heel, K1, ssk, knit to marker. You have completed the first round of gusset decreases.

Round 2 Work even on all stitches.

Next Rounds Repeat Rounds 1 and 2 until each sock contains
M 52 sts   L S 56 sts   M 60 sts

Working the Sock Feet

Continue on these stitches as established, working no further decreases, until the measurement from the back of the heel is
M 7¼″   L S 8″   M 9″
(18.5 cm)   (20.25 cm)   (22.75 cm)

or 2″ (5 cm) less than the length of the foot of the intended wearer.

Decreasing for the Toes

Note Continue the Varsity Stripe Sequence for the toe.

Set Up Work one more round, ending at the beginning of sock B sole. Move the marker from the center of sock B sole to the beginning of sock B sole, to mark the new beginning of rounds.

Round 1

- On sock B sole, K1, ssk, knit to last 3 stitches, K2tog, K1.
- On sock A sole, K1, ssk, knit to last 3 stitches, K2tog, K1.
- On sock A instep, K1, ssk, work in K3, P1 ribbing as established to last 3 stitches, K2tog, K1.
- On sock B instep, K1, ssk, knit to last 3 stitches, K2tog, K1.

Round 2 Knit all stitches.

Next Rounds Knit Rounds 1 and 2	M 5 more times	L S 6 more times	M 7 more times
Next Rounds Knit Round 1	M 5 more times	L S 5 more times	M 5 more times

Each sock now has a total of 8 stitches: 4 instep and 4 sole stitches.

Follow the Kitchener Stitch instructions on pages 28–29 to graft the toes closed.

Finishing

Weave in any loose ends. Block both socks, following the instructions on page 134.

2 -at-a-time TIP

Striping Strategies

When stripes are narrow, it's often possible to carry the color you're not using up the work as you go. When stripes are more than three rounds deep, you'll probably need to cut the yarn and attach the new color. When I made the sample for the Varsity socks, I cut my ends as I went, leaving a 4" (10 cm) tail. Once I was done with the socks, I wove in all my ends in the usual manner. Another method that can be accomplished while you knit is to weave in the yarn tails of the old color as you work the new color. In my world, there's no right or wrong way to accomplish knitted things, as long as the outcome is what you desire!

Belle Époque

The picot edging of this adorable sock is only the beginning. A centrally placed mock-cable twist bordered by open, lacy structure creates a feeling of pampered luxury. This girlie-girl sock is equally comfortable under jeans or dress pants. The feminine patterning is held within columns of ribbing for a clean look. In spite of its delicate appearance, this is a straightforward pattern to knit and incredibly rewarding to watch grow!

YARN	Louet Gems Merino Superfine, 100% merino wool, 185 yds (169 m)/1.75 oz (50) g. Yarn band gauge: 6.5–7.5 stitches = 1" (2.5 cm) in Stockinette Stitch on US 2–3 (2.75–3.25 mm) needles Teal 54: 2 skeins
GAUGE	8 stitches and 11 rows = 1" (2.5 cm) in Stockinette Stitch
NEEDLE	US 2 (2.75 mm) 40" (100 cm) long circular, *or size needed to obtain correct gauge*
NOTIONS	Stitch markers, tape measure, small cable needle, darning needle
SIZES	S Women's Small M Women's Medium L Women's Large

FINISHED FOOT CIRCUMFERENCE
- S 7½" (19 cm)
- M 8¼" (21 cm)
- L 9" (22.75 cm)

Pattern Stitches

PICOT EDGE STITCH
K2tog, YO.

RIBBING
K1, P1.

STOCKINETTE STITCH
Knit every round.

Knitting the Legs

Set Up For each sock, cast on   **S** 64 sts   **M** 72 sts   **L** 80 sts

Note If desired, attach locking stitch marker or scrap of contrasting color yarn to your work one stitch over from your join on sock A to mark the beginning of your work.

Rounds 1–5 Knit.

Round 6 *Work Picot Edge Stitch:* *K2tog, YO; repeat from * around both socks.

Rounds 7–11 Knit.

Round 12 *Turn picot edge:* Knit one live stitch on needle together with back loop of first cast-on stitch. This joins the two together and creates a finished and turned hem edge for the sock. Knit each successive live stitch together with its cast-on counterpart until the hems on both socks are completed.

Next Round

- *K1, work in P1, K1 rib for   **S** 7 sts   **M** 9 sts   **L** 11sts
- Work Belle Époque Cable Pattern (see page 61) across 18 stitches.
- K1, work in P1, K1 rib across remaining   **S** 7 sts   **M** 9 sts   **L** 11 sts
- Repeat from *.

Next Rounds

Repeat rib and charted patterns as established until leg measures   **S** 6"   **M** 6½"   **L** 7"

Note End ready to begin sock A heel. Remove any markers used to denote beginning of round, and reserve for later.

Working the Heel Flaps

Note Work the heel flaps for both socks in rows at the same time on   **S** 32 sts   **M** 36 sts   **L** 40 sts

Row 1 * Slip 1 stitch with yarn in back, K1; repeat from * to end of row.

Row 2 Slip the first stitch; purl to the end of row. (Note that the first heel flap row for sock B is Row 2.)

Next Rows Repeat Rows 1 and 2   **S** 15 more times   **M** 17 more times   **L** 19 more times

End having just worked Row 2.

	S	**M**	**L**
The heel flaps now measure about	**S** 2" (5 cm)	**M** 2¼" (5.75 cm)	**L** 2½" (6.25 cm)

Turning the Heels

Note Turn the heels on each sock separately, working in rows and beginning with sock A.

Row 1

- Knit across first   **S** 17 sts   **M** 20 sts   **L** 22 sts
- Ssk, K1, turn.

Row 2 Slip 1, P5, P2tog, P1, turn.

Row 3 Slip 1, knit to one stitch before gap, ssk to close gap, K1, turn.

Row 4 Slip 1, purl to one stitch before gap, P2tog to close gap, P1, turn.

Next Rows Repeat Rows 3 and 4 until all stitches have been worked.

Sock A heel now has   **S** 18 sts   **M** 20 sts   **L** 22 sts

Follow the directions above to turn sock B heel.

Picking Up Stitches for Gussets

Note Begin by picking up stitches on sock B heel.

Pick-Up Round

- Knit across sock B heel. Place a marker at the center of sock B heel. This represents the new beginning of rounds. With right side facing, along the left side of sock B heel pick up and knit   **S** 16 sts   **M** 18 sts   **L** 20 sts

- Move to sock A, and knit across the heel stitches.

- Along left side of sock A heel, pick up and knit   **S** 16 sts   **M** 18 sts   **L** 20 sts

- Work Belle Époque Cable Pattern as established across sock A and B instep stitches.

- Along right side of sock B heel, pick up and knit   **S** 16 sts   **M** 18 sts   **L** 20 sts

- Knit across heel stitches to marker, slide marker, work left side of sock B heel. Along right side of sock A heel, pick up and knit   **S** 16 sts   **M** 18 sts   **L** 20 sts

- Continue as established to the marker at the center of sock B heel.

Working the Gusset Decreases

Round 1

- On sock B heel, work to last 3 stitches, K2tog, K1.
- On sock A heel, K1, ssk, knit to last 3 stitches, K2tog, K1.
- Knit instep stitches in Belle Époque Cable Pattern as established on both socks. (Do not decrease on instep stitches.)
- On sock B heel, K1, ssk, knit to marker. You have completed the first round of gusset decreases.

Round 2 Work even on all stitches.

Next Rounds Repeat Rounds 1 and 2 until each sock contains
   S 64 sts   **M** 72 sts   **L** 80 sts

Working the Sock Feet

Continue on these stitches as established, working no further decreases, until the measurement from the back of the heel is

   S 7¼"   **M** 7½"   **L** 8"
      (18.25 cm)   (19 cm)   (20.25 cm)

or 1½" (3.75 cm) less than the length of the foot of the intended wearer.

Decreasing for the Toes

Set Up Work one more round, ending at the beginning of sock B sole. Move the marker from the center of sock B sole to the beginning of sock B sole, to mark the new beginning of rounds.

Round 1

- On sock B sole, K1, ssk, knit to last 3 stitches, K2tog, K1.
- On sock A sole, K1, ssk, knit to last 3 stitches, K2tog, K1.
- On sock A instep, K1, ssk, knit to last 3 stitches, K2tog, K1.
- On sock B instep, K1, ssk, knit to last 3 stitches, K2tog, K1.

Round 2 Knit all stitches.

		S	M	L
Next Rounds	Repeat Rounds 1 and 2	6 more times	7 more times	8 more times
Next Rounds	Repeat Round 1	6 more times	6 more times	7 more times

Each sock now has a total of 16 stitches: 8 instep and 8 sole stitches.

Follow the Kitchener Stitch instructions on pages 28–29 to graft the toes closed.

Finishing

Weave in any loose ends. Block both socks, following the instructions on page 134.

BELLE ÉPOQUE CABLE PATTERN

18	17	16	15	14	13	12	11	10	9	8	7	6	5	4	3	2	1	

(Chart rows numbered 8 down to 1 on the right.)

key

- ☐ Knit
- • Purl
- ╱ Knit 2 together
- ○ Yarn over
- ⊠ Slip 3 stitches onto right-hand needle, knit into the front and back of the next stitch, K2, pass 3 slipped stitches over 4 stitches just worked

Frolic

This sock allows for some experimentation with cables without the commitment of fingering weight yarn or adult sizing. And, you get an adorable, washable kids' sock perfect for gift-giving. Yarn with an excellent twist gives this cable pattern great stitch definition.

YARN Louet Gems Merino Sport Weight, 100% merino wool, 3½ oz (100 g)/225 yds (206 m). Yarn band gauge: 5–6 stitches = 1" (2.5 cm)
Crabapple 26: **S** 1 skein; **M** 2 skeins; **L** 2 skeins

GAUGE 6 stitches and 8 rows = 1" (2.5 cm) in Stockinette Stitch

NEEDLE US 4 (3.5 mm) 40" (100 cm) circular, *or size needed to obtain correct gauge*

NOTIONS Stitch markers, tape measure, small cable needle, darning needle

SIZES **S** Child's Small: 2–4
M Child's Medium: 6–8
L Child's Large: 10–12

FINISHED FOOT CIRCUMFERENCE
S 5¼" (13.5 cm)
M 6¾" (17.25 cm)
L 7¼" (18.5 cm)

Pattern Stitches

RIBBING
K1, P1

STOCKINETTE STITCH
Knit every round.

Knitting the Legs

Set Up For each sock, cast on   **S** 32 sts   **M** 40 sts   **L** 44 sts
Work in K1, P1 rib for 1½" (3.75 cm).

Work the Frolic Cable Pattern (see page 67) on each sock twice in each round
until leg measurement is   **S** 4"   **M** 5"   **L** 6"
(10 cm)   (12.75 cm)   (15.25 cm)

Note End ready to begin sock A heel. Remove any markers used to denote beginning of round, and reserve for later.

Working the Heel Flaps

Note Work the heel flaps for both socks in rows at the same time on
S 16 sts   **M** 20 sts   **L** 22 sts

Row 1 *Slip 1 stitch with yarn in back, K1; repeat from * to end of row.

Row 2 Slip the first stitch; purl to the end of row. (Note that the first heel flap row for sock B is Row 2.)

Next Rows Repeat Rows 1 and 2   **S** 7   **M** 8   **L** 9
more   more   more
times   times   times

End having just worked Row 2.

The heel flaps now measure about   **S** 1"   **M** 1½"   **L** 1¾"
(2.5 cm)   (3.75 cm)   (4.5 cm)

Turning the Heels

Note Turn the heel on each sock separately, beginning with sock A.

Row 1

- Knit across first   **S** 10 sts   **M** 12 sts   **L** 13 sts
- Ssk, K1, turn.

Row 2 Slip 1, P5, P2tog, P1, turn.

Row 3 Slip 1, knit to one stitch before gap, ssk to close gap, K1, turn.

Row 4 Slip 1, purl to one stitch before gap, P2tog to close gap, P1, turn.

Next Rows Repeat Rows 3 and 4 until all stitches have been worked.

Sock A heel now has   **S** 10 sts   **M** 12 sts   **L** 13 sts

Follow directions above to turn sock B heel.

Picking Up Stitches for Gussets

Note Begin by picking up stitches on sock B heel.

Pick-Up Round

- Knit across sock B heel. Place a marker at the center of sock B heel. This represents the new beginning of rounds. With right side facing, along the left side of sock B heel pick up and knit

      S 8 sts   **M** 9 sts   **L** 10 sts

- Move to sock A, and knit across the heel stitches.

- Along left side of sock A heel, pick up and knit

      S 8 sts   **M** 9 sts   **L** 10 sts

- Work Frolic Cable Pattern as established on socks A and B instep stitches.

- Along right side of sock B heel, pick up and knit

      S 8 sts   **M** 9 sts   **L** 10 sts

- Knit across sock B heel stitches to marker, slip marker, work left side of sock B heel. Along right side of sock A heel, pick up and knit

      S 8 sts   **M** 9 sts   **L** 10 sts

- Continue as established to the marker at the center of sock B heel.

Working the Gusset Decreases

Round 1

- Work to last 3 stitches of sock B heel, K2tog, K1.

- On sock A heel, K1, ssk, knit to last 3 stitches, K2tog, K1.

- Knit instep stitches on both socks. (Don't decrease on the instep stitches.)

- On sock B heel, K1, ssk, knit to marker. You have completed the first round of gusset decreases.

Round 2 Work as established on all stitches.

Next Rounds Repeat Rounds 1 and 2 until each sock contains

    S 32 sts   **M** 40 sts   **L** 44 sts

Working the Sock Feet

Continue on these stitches as established, working no further decreases, until the measurement from the back of the heel is

S 3" **M** 4" **L** 5"
(7.5 cm) (10 cm) (12.75 cm)

or 1½" (3.75 cm) less than the length of the foot of the intended wearer.

Decreasing for the Toes

Set Up Work one more round, ending at the beginning of sock B sole. Move the marker from the center of sock B sole to the beginning of sock B sole, to mark the new beginning of rounds.

Round 1

- On sock B sole, K1, ssk, knit to last 3 stitches, K2tog, K1.
- On sock A sole, K1, ssk, knit to last 3 stitches, K2tog, K1.
- On sock A instep, K1, ssk, knit to last 3 stitches, K2tog, K1.
- On sock B instep, K1, ssk, knit to last 3 stitches, K2tog, K1.

Round 2 Knit all stitches.

Next Rounds Knit Rounds 1 and 2   **S** 5   **M** 7   **L** 8
more   more   more
times   times   times

Each sock now has a total of 8 stitches: 4 instep and 4 sole stitches.

Follow the Kitchener Stitch instructions on pages 28–29 to graft the toes closed.

Finishing

Weave in any loose ends. Block both socks, following the instructions on page 134.

FROLIC CABLE PATTERN

Column size markers (left to right): **10–12** (col 22), **6–8** (col 21), **2–4** (col 20) … **2–4** (col 3), **6–8** (col 2), **10–12** (col 1)

22	21	20	19	18	17	16	15	14	13	12	11	10	9	8	7	6	5	4	3	2	1	Row
•	•	•	•	•													•	•	•	•	•	16
•	•	•	•	•													•	•	•	•	•	15
•	•	•	•	•	X	X	X	X	X	X	X	X	X	X	X	X	•	•	•	•	•	14
•	•	•	•	•													•	•	•	•	•	13
•	•	•	•	•													•	•	•	•	•	12
•	•	•	•	•													•	•	•	•	•	11
•	•	•	•	•				•	•	•	•	•	•	•	•		•	•	•	•	•	10
•	•	•	•	•				•	•	•	•	•	•	•	•		•	•	•	•	•	9
•	•	•	•	•													•	•	•	•	•	8
•	•	•	•	•													•	•	•	•	•	7
•	•	•	•	•													•	•	•	•	•	6
•	•	•	•	•	X	X	X	X	X	X	X	X	X	X	X	X	•	•	•	•	•	5
•	•	•	•	•				•	•	•	•	•	•				•	•	•	•	•	4
•	•	•	•	•				•	•	•	•	•	•				•	•	•	•	•	3
•	•	•	•	•				•	•	•	•	•	•				•	•	•	•	•	2
•	•	•	•	•				•	•	•	•	•	•				•	•	•	•	•	1

key

☐ Knit

• Purl

⬒ Slip 3 stitches to cable needle and hold to back, K3, K3 from cable needle

⬒ Slip 3 stitches to cable needle and hold to front, K3, K3 from cable needle

Coquette

There's something captivating about bamboo yarn and the iridescent glow it creates. These flirty little anklets are perfect for summer, with an open stitch pattern and a very gentle ruffle at the cuff. Knitting with bamboo can be challenging: The long fibers want to escape when you slip some stitches over others in the pattern. Persevere, knitter — the results are well worth the labor!

YARN	Regia Bamboo Color, 45% bamboo/40% new wool/15% polyamide, fingering weight, 1¾ oz (50 g)/219 yds (200 m). Yarn ball gauge: 7.5 stitches = 1″ (2.5 cm) on US 0-2 (2 mm–2.75 mm) needles. Jaffa 1072: 2 skeins
GAUGE	8 stitches and 11 rows = 1″ (2.5 cm) in Stockinette Stitch
NEEDLE	US 1 (2.5 mm) 40″ (100 cm) circular, *or size needed to obtain correct gauge*
NOTIONS	Stitch markers, tape measure, darning needle
SIZES	**S** Women's Small **M** Women's Medium **L** Women's Large

FINISHED FOOT CIRCUMFERENCE
- **S** 7½″ (19 cm)
- **M** 8¼″ (21 cm)
- **L** 9″ (22.75 cm)

Pattern Stitches

STOCKINETTE STITCH
Knit every round.

COQUETTE STITCH PATTERN
ROUND 1 *P3, yo, K3tog,yo; repeat from * around both socks.
ROUNDS 2–4 *P3, K3; repeat from * around both socks.

Getting Started

Set up For each sock, cast on   **S** 120 sts   **M** 132 sts   **L** 144 sts

Note If desired, attach locking stitch marker or scrap of contrasting color yarn one stitch past join on sock A to mark the beginning of your work.

Knitting the Legs

Ruffled Edge *P2tog three times, K2tog three times; repeat from * around both socks. Each sock now contains   **S** 60 sts   **M** 66 sts   **L** 72 sts

Next Rows Beginning with Coquette Stitch Pattern (see page 73) Round 3, work in pattern until leg measures   **S** 3½″ (9 cm)   **M** 3½″ (9 cm)   **L** 4″ (10 cm)

Note End ready to begin sock A heel. Remove any markers used to denote beginning of round, and reserve for later.

Working the Heel Flaps

Note Work the heel flaps for both socks in rows at the same time on   **S** 30 sts   **M** 33 sts   **L** 36 sts

Row 1 *Slip 1 stitch with yarn in back, K1; repeat from * to end of row.

Row 2 Slip the first stitch, purl to end of row. (Note that the first heel flap row for sock B is Row 2.)

Next Rows Repeat Rows 1 and 2   **S** 14 more times   **M** 15 more times   **L** 17 more times

End having just worked Row 2.

The heel flaps now measure about   **S** 2″ (5 cm)   **M** 2¼″ (5.75 cm)   **L** 2½″ (6.25 cm)

Turning the Heels

Note Turn heels separately, working in rows and beginning with sock A.

Row 1

- Knit   **S** 17 sts   **M** 18 sts   **L** 20 sts
- Ssk, K1, turn.

Row 2 Slip 1, P5, P2tog, P1, turn.

Row 3 Slip 1, knit to one stitch before gap, ssk to close gap, K1, turn.

Row 4 Slip 1, purl to one stitch before gap, P2tog, P1, turn.

Next Rows Repeat Rows 3 and 4 until all stitches have been worked.

Sock A heel now has   **S** 17 sts   **M** 19 sts   **L** 20 sts

Follow directions above to turn sock B heel.

Picking Up Stitches for Gussets

Note Begin by picking up stitches on sock B heel.

Pick-Up Round

- Knit across sock B heel. Place a marker at the center of sock B heel. This represents the new beginning of rounds. With right side facing and working along the left side of sock B heel, pick up and knit
     S 15 sts   **M** 16 sts   **L** 18 sts

- Move to sock A, and knit across the heel stitches.

- Along left side of sock A heel, pick up and knit
     S 15 sts   **M** 16 sts   **L** 18 sts

- Knit across sock A and B instep stitches.

- Along right side of sock B heel, pick up and knit
     S 15 sts   **M** 16 sts   **L** 18 sts

- Knit across sock B heel stitches to marker, slip marker, work left side of sock B heel. On right side of sock A heel, pick up and knit
     S 15 sts   **M** 16 sts   **L** 18 sts

- Continue as established to the marker at the center of sock B heel.

Working the Gusset Decreases

Round 1

- On sock B heel, work to last 3, K2tog, K1.

- On sock A heel, K1, ssk, knit to last 3 stitches, K2tog, K1.

- Knit instep stitches on both socks. (Don't decrease on instep stitches.)

- On sock B heel, K1, ssk, knit to marker. You have completed the first round of gusset decreases.

Round 2 Work even on all stitches.

Next Rounds Repeat Rounds 1 and 2 until each sock contains

S 60 sts   **M** 66 sts   **L** 72 sts

Working the Sock Feet

Continue on these stitches as established, working no further decreases, until the measurement from the back of the heel is

S 7″   **M** 7½″   **L** 8″
(17.75 cm)   (19 cm)   (20.25 cm)

or 1½″ (3.75 cm) less than the length of the foot of the intended wearer.

Decreasing for the Toes

Set Up Work one more round, ending at the beginning of sock B sole. Move the marker from the center of sock B sole to the beginning of sock B sole, to mark the new beginning of rounds.

Round 1

- On sock B sole, K1, ssk, knit to the last 3 stitches, K2tog, K1.
- On sock A sole, K1, ssk, knit to last 3 stitches, K2tog, K1.
- On sock A instep, K1, ssk, knit to last 3 stitches, K2tog, K1.
- On sock B instep, K1, ssk, knit to last 3 stitches, K2tog, K1.

Round 2 Knit all stitches.

Next Rounds Repeat Rounds 1 and 2

S 5 more times   **M** 6 more times   **L** 7 more times

Next Rounds Repeat Round 1

S 5 more times   **M** 6 more times   **L** 6 more times

The instep and sole of each sock now has

S 8 sts   **M** 7 sts   **L** 8 sts

Each sock now has a total of

S 16 sts   **M** 14 sts   **L** 16 sts

Follow the Kitchener Stitch instructions on pages 28–29 to graft toe closed.

Finishing

Weave in any loose ends. Block both socks, following the instructions on page 134.

COQUETTE STITCH PATTERN

			•	•	•	4
			•	•	•	3
			•	•	•	2
○	人	○	•	•	•	1
6	5	4	3	2	1	

key

☐	Knit
•	Purl
人	Knit 3 together
○	Yarn over

Socks for Aidan

The best gifts are the ones you're not expecting. When we found out that we were to be grandparents for the first time, we were a little nervous. After all, we're not old enough to be grandparents, are we? It's been three years, and I think we've adjusted. I am amazed that one small person can bring so much into your life and teach you so very much about yourself. These socks are for the boy who made us realize that age is relative — oh, and that being a grandparent is the coolest job in the world.

YARN Lang Jawoll solids, 75% new wool/ 18% nylon/7% acrylic,), 1½ oz (50 g)/230 (210 m). Yarn band gauge: 7½ stitches = 1" (2.5 cm) in stockinette stitch on 0–2 US (2–3 mm).
MC = 25 (navy blue): 1 skein
CA = 01 (white): 1 skein
CB = 33 (medium blue): 1 skein
CC = 03 (gray): 1 skein

GAUGE 8 stitches and 10 rows = 1" (2.5 cm) in Stockinette Stitch

NEEDLE US 1 (2.5 mm) 40" (100 cm) circular, *or size needed to obtain correct gauge*

NOTIONS Stitch markers, tape measure, darning needle

SIZES
- S Child's Small: 2–4
- M Child's Medium: 6–8
- L Child's Large: 10–12

FINISHED FOOT CIRCUMFERENCE
- S 4½" (11.5 cm)
- M 6" (15.25 cm)
- L 7½" (19 cm)

Pattern Stitches

RIBBING
K2, P2
K1, P1

STOCKINETTE STITCH
Knit every round.

GARTER STITCH
ROUND 1 Knit.

Knitting the Legs

Set Up For each sock, using MC, cast on **S** 36 sts **M** 48 sts **L** 60 sts

Note If desired, attach locking stitch marker or scrap of contrasting color yarn to your work one stitch over from your join on sock A to mark the beginning of your work.

Rounds 1–4 Work in K1, P1 rib.

Rounds 5–19 Starting with CA, work one full repeat of Socks for Aidan Color Chart (see page 79) **S** 6 times per round **M** 8 times per round **L** 10 times per round

Rounds 20–23 Change to MC and work K1, P1 rib.

Round 24 Knit.

Round 25 Purl.

Note Rounds 24 and 25 will create a turning ridge.

Turning Round Turn your sock cuffs inside out, so the wrong side of the stranded colorwork is facing you. Continue working in the round. You are reversing direction, creating a very small hole that can be left alone or closed later with a scrap of yarn.

Next Rounds In MC, work in K2, P2 rib until measurement from cast-on edge is **S** 4" (10 cm) **M** 4½" (11.5 cm) **L** 4½" (11.5 cm)

Note End ready to begin sock A heel. Remove any markers used to denote beginning of round, and reserve for later.

Working the Heel Flaps

Note Work the heel flaps for both socks in rows at the same time on **S** 18 sts **M** 24 sts **L** 30 sts

Row 1 *Slip 1 stitch with yarn in back, K1; repeat from * to end of row.

Row 2 Slip the first stitch; purl to the end of row. (Note that the first heel flap row for sock B is Row 2.)

Next Rows Repeat Rows 1 and 2	S 7 more times	M 8 more times	L 11 more times

End having just worked Row 2.

The heel flaps now measure about	S 1" (2.5 cm)	M 1½" (3.75 cm)	L 1¾" (4.5 cm)

Turning the Heels

Note Turn the heel on each sock separately, beginning with sock A.

Row 1

- Knit across first S 11 sts M 14 sts L 17 sts
- Ssk, K1, turn.

Row 2 Slip 1, P5, P2tog, P1, turn.

Row 3 Slip 1, knit to one stitch before gap, ssk to close gap, K1, turn.

Row 4 Slip 1, purl to one stitch before gap, P2tog to close gap, P1, turn.

Next Rows Repeat Rows 3 and 4 until all stitches have been worked.

Sock A heel now has S 11 sts M 14 sts L 17 sts

Follow directions above to turn sock B heel.

Picking Up Stitches for Gussets

Note Begin by picking up stitches on sock B heel.

Pick-Up Round

- In MC, knit across sock B heel. Place a marker at the center of sock B heel. This represents the new beginning of rounds. With right side facing, along the left side of sock B heel pick up and knit

  S 8 sts M 9 sts L 12 sts

- Move to sock A, and knit across the heel stitches.
- Along left side of sock A heel, pick up and knit

  S 8 sts M 9 sts L 12 sts

- Work K2, P2 ribbing as established across sock A and B instep stitches.
- Along right side of sock B heel, pick up and knit

  S 8 sts M 9 sts L 12 sts

- Knit across sock B heel stitches to marker, slip marker, work left side of sock B heel. Along right side of sock A heel, pick up and knit
  S 8 sts   **M** 9 sts   **L** 12 sts

Continue working both socks as established until you return to the marker placed at the center of sock B heel.

Working the Gusset Decreases

Round 1

- On sock B heel, work to last 3 stitches, K2tog, K1.

- On sock A heel, K1, ssk, knit to last 3 stitches, K2tog, K1.

- Knit instep stitches in K2, P2 ribbing on both socks. (Don't decrease on the instep stitches.)

- On sock B heel, K1, ssk, knit to marker. You have completed the first round of gusset decreases.

Round 2 Work even on all stitches.

Next Rounds Repeat Rounds 1 and 2 until each sock contains
  S 36 sts   **M** 48 sts   **L** 60 sts

Working the Sock Feet

Continue on these stitches as established, working no further decreases, until the measurement from the back of the heel is
  S 2½"   **M** 4"   **L** 5"
  (7.5 cm)   (10 cm)   (12.75 cm)

or 1½" (3.75 cm) less than the length of the foot of the intended wearer.

Decreasing for the Toes

Set Up Work one more round, ending at the beginning of sock B sole. Move the marker from the center of sock B sole to the beginning of sock B sole, to mark the new beginning of rounds.

Round 1

- On sock B sole, K1, ssk, knit to last 3 stitches, K2tog, K1.

- On sock A sole, K1, ssk, knit to last 3 stitches, K2tog, K1.

- On sock A instep, K1, ssk, knit to last 3 stitches, K2tog, K1.
- On sock B instep, K1, ssk, knit to last 3 stitches, K2tog, K1.

Round 2 Knit all stitches.

Next Rounds Knit Rounds 1 and 2   **S** 3 more times   **M** 5 more times   **L** 6 more times

Next Rounds Knit Round 1   **S** 3 more times   **M** 4 more times   **L** 6 more times

Each sock now has a total of 8 stitches: 4 instep and 4 sole stitches.

Follow the Kitchener Stitch instructions on pages 28–29 to graft toe closed.

Finishing

Weave in any loose ends. Block both socks, following the instructions on page 134.

SOCKS FOR AIDAN COLOR CHART

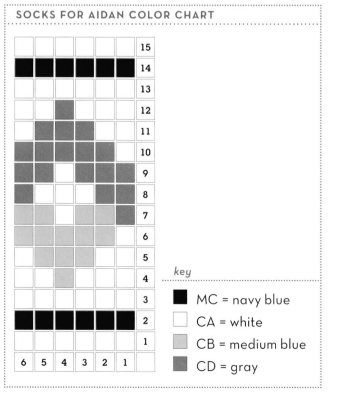

key

■ MC = navy blue

□ CA = white

▨ CB = medium blue

▨ CD = gray

Twilight

This sock whispers of that magic hour between day and night — my favorite time of day, when the light never ceases to surprise me with its colors. Sitting on the deck in the evening watching the stars come out one by one and the last bit of daylight fade from the sky is amazingly soothing. The rhythmic pattern of this sock works especially well with hand-painted yarns, texture accenting the color just as the outlines of trees and branches stand out in the dwindling evening light.

YARN	Valley Yarns Kangaroo Dyer Franklin, 75% wool/25% nylon, fingering weight, 4 oz (113 g)/450 yds (411 m). Yarn band gauge 7–8 stitches = 1" (2.5 cm) in Stockinette Stitch on US 0–2 (2–2.75 mm) needles. Twilight: 1 skein
GAUGE	8 stitches and 10 rows = 1" (2.5 cm) in Stockinette Stitch
NEEDLE	US 1 (2.5 mm) 40" (100 cm) circular, or size needed to obtain correct gauge
NOTIONS	Stitch markers, tape measure, darning needle
SIZES	M Women's Medium LS Women's Large/Men's Small M Men's Medium

FINISHED FOOT CIRCUMFERENCE
- M 8" (20.25 cm)
- LS 9" (22.75 cm)
- M 9½" (24.25 cm)

Pattern Stitches

RIBBING
K1, P3.

STOCKINETTE STITCH
Knit every round.

TWILIGHT STITCH PATTERN
ROUNDS 1 AND 2 K1, P3.
ROUNDS 3–6 Knit.

Knitting the Legs

Set Up For each sock, cast on **M** 64 sts **LS** 72 sts **M** 76 sts

Note If desired, attach locking stitch marker or scrap of contrasting color yarn to your work one stitch over from your join on sock A to mark the beginning of your work.

Work in K1, P3 rib for 2″ (5 cm).

Work Twilight Stitch Pattern (see page 85) until leg measurement from cast-on edge is **M** 6″ **LS** 7″ **M** 8″
(15.25 cm) (17.75 cm) (20.25 cm)

Note End ready to begin sock A heel. Remove any markers used to denote beginning of round, and reserve for later.

Working the Heel Flaps

Note Work the heel flaps for both socks in rows at the same time on **M** 32 sts **LS** 36 sts **M** 38 sts

Row 1 *Slip 1 stitch with yarn in back, K1; repeat from * to end of row.

Row 2 Slip the first stitch; purl to the end of row. (Note that the first heel flap row for sock B is Row 2.)

Next Rows Repeat Rows 1 and 2 **M** 16 **LS** 17 **M** 18
more more more
times times times

End having just worked Row 2.

The heel flaps now measure about **M** 2″ **LS** 2¼″ **M** 2½″
(5 cm) (5.75 cm) (6.25 cm)

Turning the Heels

Note Turn the heel on each sock separately, beginning with sock A.

Row 1

- Knit across first **M** 17 sts **LS** 20 sts **M** 21 sts
- Ssk, K1, turn.

Row 2 Slip 1, P5, P2tog, P1, turn.

Row 3 Slip 1, knit to one stitch before gap, ssk to close gap, K1, turn.

Row 4 Slip 1, purl to one stitch before gap, P2tog to close gap, P1, turn.

Next Rows Repeat Rows 3 and 4 until all stitches have been worked.

Sock A heel now has   **M** 18 sts   **LS** 20 sts   **M** 22 sts

Follow directions above to turn sock B heel.

Picking Up Stitches for Gussets

Note Begin by picking up stitches on left side of sock B heel.

Pick-Up Round

- Knit across sock B heel. Place a marker at the center of sock B heel. This represents the new beginning of rounds. With right side facing, along the left side of sock B heel pick up and knit

       M 17 sts   **LS** 18 sts   **M** 19 sts

- Move to sock A, and knit across the heel stitches.

- Along left side of sock A heel, pick up and knit

       M 17 sts   **LS** 18 sts   **M** 19 sts

- Work in Twilight Stitch Pattern as established across sock A and B instep stitches.

- Along right side of sock B heel, pick up and knit

       M 17 sts   **LS** 18 sts   **M** 19 sts

- Knit across sock B heel stitches to marker, slip marker, work left side of sock B heel. Along right side of sock A heel, pick up and knit

       M 17 sts   **LS** 18 sts   **M** 19 sts

- Continue as established to the marker at the center of sock B heel.

Working the Gusset Decreases

Round 1

- On sock B heel, work to last 3 stitches, K2tog, K1.

- On sock A heel, K1, ssk, knit to last 3 stitches, K2tog, K1.

- Work instep stitches in Twilight Stitch Pattern on both socks as established. (Don't decrease on the instep stitches.)

- On sock B heel, K1, ssk, knit to marker. You have completed the first round of gusset decreases.

Round 2 Work even on all stitches.

Next Rounds Repeat Rounds 1 and 2 until each sock contains

M 64 sts   LS 72 sts   M 76 sts

Working the Sock Feet

Continue on these stitches as established, working no further decreases, until the measurement from the back of the heel is

M 7¾"   LS 8½"   M 9½"
(19.75 cm)   (21.5 cm)   (24.25 cm)

or 1½" (3.75 cm) less than the length of the foot of the intended wearer.

Decreasing for the Toes

Set Up Work one more round, ending at the beginning of sock B sole. Move the marker from the center of sock B sole to the beginning of sock B sole, to mark the new beginning of rounds.

Round 1

- On sock B sole, K1, ssk, knit to last 3 stitches, K2tog, K1.
- On sock A sole, K1, ssk, knit to last 3 stitches, K2tog, K1.
- On sock A instep, K1, ssk, knit to last 3 stitches, K2tog, K1.
- On sock B instep, K1, ssk, knit to last 3 stitches, K2tog, K1.

Round 2 Knit all stitches.

Next Rounds Knit Rounds 1 and 2   M 6 more times   LS 7 more times   M 8 more times

Next Rounds Knit Round 1   M 6 more times   LS 6 more times   M 6 more times

Each sock now has a total of 16 stitches: 8 instep and 8 sole stitches.

Follow the Kitchener Stitch instructions on pages 28–29 to graft toe closed.

Finishing

Weave in any loose ends. Block both socks, following the instructions on page 134.

TWILIGHT STITCH PATTERN

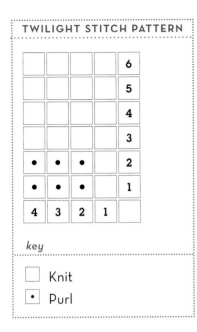

key

☐ Knit
⊡ Purl

Sugar Maple

This sock is designed with hand-painted yarns in mind: It gives the hands something to do every few rounds without creating competition between the stitches and the colors. Knit in rich, autumnal colors, the columns of twisting stitches make me think of changing maple trees in autumn. Nothing tops foliage season in New England!

YARN Valley Yarns Kangaroo Dyer Franklin, 75% wool/25% nylon. 4 oz (113 g)/450 yds (411 m). Yarn band gauge: 7–8 stitches = 1″ (2.5 cm) in Stockinette Stitch on US 0–2 (2–2.75 mm) needles.
Chutney: 1 skein

GAUGE 8 stitches and 10 rows = 1″ (2.5 cm) in Stockinette Stitch

NEEDLE US 1 (2.5 mm) 40″ (100 cm) circular, *or size that you need to obtain correct gauge*

NOTIONS Stitch markers, tape measure, darning needle

SIZES
S Women's Small
M Women's Medium
L Women's Large

FINISHED FOOT CIRCUMFERENCE
S 8″ (20.25 cm)
M 8½″ (21.5 cm)
L 9″ (22.75 cm)

Pattern Stitches

STOCKINETTE STITCH
Knit every round

SUGAR MAPLE STITCH PATTERN
ROUND 1 P2, K1tbl of second stitch on left-hand needle, leave on needle, knit into first stitch, move both stitches to right-hand needle.
ROUNDS 2 AND 3 P2, K2.

Knitting the Legs

Set Up For each sock, cast on **S** 68 sts **M** 72 sts **L** 76 sts

Note If desired, attach locking stitch marker or scrap of contrasting color yarn one stitch past join on sock A to mark the beginning of your work.

Rounds 1 and 2 P2, K2 to end of each round.

Next Rounds Work in Sugar Maple Stitch (see page 91) until leg measurement from cast-on edge is **S** 6" **M** 6½" **L** 7"
(15.25 cm) (16.5 cm) (17.75 cm)

Note End ready to begin sock A heel. Remove any markers used to denote beginning of rounds, and reserve for later.

Working the Heel Flaps

Note Work the heel flaps for both socks in rows at the same time on **S** 34 sts **M** 36 sts **L** 38 sts

Row 1 *Slip 1 stitch with yarn in back, K1; repeat from * to end of row.

Row 2 Slip the first stitch; purl to the end of row. (Note that the first heel flap row for sock B is Row 2.)

Next Rows Repeat Rows 1 and 2 **S** 15 **M** 16 **L** 17
more more more
times times times

End having just worked Row 2.

The heel flaps now measure about **S** 2" **M** 2¼" **L** 2½"
(5 cm) (5.75 cm) (6.25 cm)

Turning the Heels

Note Turn the heel on each sock separately, beginning with sock A.

Row 1

- Knit across first **S** 18 sts **M** 20 sts **L** 21 sts
- Ssk, K1, turn.

Row 2 Slip 1, P5, P2tog, P1, turn.

Row 3 Slip 1, knit to one stitch before gap, ssk to close gap, K1, turn.

Row 4 Slip 1, purl to one stitch before gap, P2tog to close gap, P1, turn.

Next Rows Repeat Rows 3 and 4 until all stitches have been worked.

Sock A heel now has   **S** 19 sts   **M** 20 sts   **L** 22 sts

Follow directions above to turn sock B heel.

Picking Up Stitches for Gussets

Note Begin by picking up stitches on sock B heel.

Pick-Up Round

- Knit across sock B heel. Place a marker at the center of sock B heel. This represents the new beginning of rounds. With right side facing, along the left side of sock B heel pick up and knit

  S 16 sts   **M** 17 sts   **L** 18 sts

- Move to sock A, and knit across the heel stitches.

- Along left side of sock A heel, pick up and knit

  S 16 sts   **M** 17 sts   **L** 18 sts

- Work Sugar Maple Stitch as established across sock A and B instep stitches.

- Along right side of sock B heel, pick up and knit

  S 16 sts   **M** 17 sts   **L** 18 sts

- Knit across sock B heel stitches to marker, slip marker, work left side of sock B heel. Along right side of sock A heel, pick up and knit

  S 16 sts   **M** 17 sts   **L** 18 sts

- Continue as established to the marker at the center of sock B heel.

Working the Gusset Decreases

Round 1

- On sock B heel, knit to last 3 stitches, K2tog, K1.

- On sock A heel, K1, ssk, knit to last 3 stitches, K2tog, K1.

- Work instep stitches in Sugar Maple Stitch as established on both socks. (Don't decrease on the instep stitches.)

- On sock B heel, K1, ssk, knit to marker. You have completed the first round of gusset decreases.

Round 2 Work even on all stitches.

 *Sugar Maple* (cont'd)   **S** W's S   **M** W's M   **L** W's L

Next Rounds Repeat Rounds 1 and 2 until each sock contains
S 68 sts   **M** 72 sts   **L** 76 sts

Working the Sock Feet

Continue on these stitches as established, working no further decreases, until the measurement from the back of heel is

S 6½"   **M** 7"   **L** 7¼"
(16.5 cm)   (17.75 cm)   (18.5 cm)

or 1½" (3.75 cm) less than the length of the foot of the intended wearer.

Decreasing for the Toes

Set Up Work one more round, ending at the beginning of sock B sole. Move the marker from the center of sock B sole to the beginning of sock B sole, to mark the new beginning of rounds.

Round 1

- On sock B sole, K1, ssk, knit to last 3 stitches, K2tog, K1.
- On sock A sole, K1, ssk, knit to last 3 stitches, K2tog, K1.
- On sock A instep, K1, ssk, knit to last 3 stitches, K2tog, K1.
- On sock B instep, K1, ssk, knit to last 3 stitches, K2tog, K1.

Round 2 Knit all stitches.

Next Rounds Knit Rounds 1 and 2   **S** 6 more times   **M** 7 more times   **L** 7 more times

Next Rounds Knit Round 1   **S** 6 more times   **M** 6 more times   **L** 7 more times

Each sock now has a total of 16 stitches: 8 instep and 8 sole stitches.

Follow the Kitchener Stitch instructions on pages 28–29 to graft the toes closed.

Finishing

Weave in any loose ends. Block both socks, following the instructions on page 134.

SUGAR MAPLE STITCH CHART

		•	•	3
		•	•	2
✕		•	•	1
4	3	2	1	

key

☐ Knit

• Purl

✕ Knit 1 through back loop of second stitch and leave on left-hand needle, knit into first stitch and move both stitches to right-hand needle

H Sock

These socks are "H" for two reasons: The stitch pattern creates an "H" shape, and they are the perfect House sock! Knitted in a soft, thick worsted, these will keep your feet blissfully warm on even the coldest of days. The simple knit and purl combination creates visual interest, but lets the amazing depth of color shine through. (I believe in letting the yarn do the work while giving myself a little patterning to keep my interest.)

YARN — Lorna's Laces Shepherd Worsted, 100% superwash wool, 4 oz (113 g)/225 yards (206 m). Yarn band gauge: 4.5 stitches = 1" (2.5 cm) on US 7 (4.5 mm) needles. Vera 70: 1 skein

GAUGE — 6 stitches and 8 rows = 1" (2.5 cm) in Stockinette Stitch

NEEDLE — US 4 (3.5 mm) 40" (100 cm) circular, or *size needed to obtain correct gauge*

NOTIONS — Stitch markers, tape measure, darning needle

SIZES
- S Women's Small
- M Women's Medium
- L Women's Large

FINISHED FOOT CIRCUMFERENCE
- S 8" (20.25 cm)
- M 9" (22.75 cm)
- L 10" (25.5 cm)

Pattern Stitches

RIBBING
K3, P3.

STOCKINETTE STITCH
Knit every round.

H SOCK STITCH PATTERN
ROWS 1 AND 3 K3, P1, K1, P1.
ROW 2 K3, P3.
ROWS 4 AND 8 K6.
ROWS 5 AND 7 P1, K1, P1, K3.
ROW 6 P3, K3.

Knitting the Legs

Set Up For each sock, cast on   **S** 48 sts   **M** 54 sts   **L** 60 sts

Note If desired, attach locking stitch marker or scrap of contrasting color yarn one stitch past join on sock A to mark the beginning of your work.

Work in K3, P3 rib for 2″ (5 cm).

Work in H Sock Stitch (see page 97) until leg measures

	S 6″	**M** 7″	**L** 7½″
	(15.25 cm)	(17.75 cm)	(19 cm)

Note End ready to begin sock A heel. Remove any markers used to denote beginning of round, and reserve for later.

Working the Heel Flaps

Note Work the heel flaps for both socks in rows at the same time on   **S** 24 sts   **M** 27 sts   **L** 30 sts

Row 1 *Slip 1 stitch with yarn in back, K1; repeat from * to end of row.

Row 2 Slip the first stitch, purl to end of row. (Note that the first heel flap row for sock B is Row 2.)

Next Rows Repeat Rows 1 and 2

S 11	**M** 12	**L** 14
more times	more times	more times

End having just worked Row 2.

The heel flaps now measure about

S 2″	**M** 2¼″	**L** 2½″
(5 cm)	(5.75 cm)	(6.25 cm)

Turning the Heels

Note Turn heels separately, working in rows and beginning with sock A.

Row 1

■ Knit   **S** 14 sts   **M** 15 sts   **L** 17 sts

■ Ssk, K1, turn.

Row 2 Slip 1, P5, P2tog, P1, turn.

Row 3 Slip 1, knit to one stitch before gap, ssk to close gap, K1, turn.

Row 4 Slip 1, purl to one stitch before gap, P2tog, P1, turn.

Next Rows Repeat Rows 3 and 4 until all stitches have been worked.

Sock A heel now has **S** 14 sts **M** 15 sts **L** 17 sts

Follow directions above to turn sock B heel.

Picking Up Stitches for Gussets

Note Begin by picking up stitches on sock B heel.

Pick-Up Round

- Knit across sock B heel. Place a marker at the center of sock B heel. This represents the new beginning of rounds. With right side facing, along the left side of sock B heel pick up and knit
  S 12 sts **M** 13 st **L** 15 sts

- Move to sock A, and knit across the heel stitches.

- Along left side of sock A heel, pick up and knit
  S 12 sts **M** 13 sts **L** 15 sts

- Work sock A and B instep stitches in H Sock Stitch Pattern as established.

- Along right side of sock B heel, pick up and knit
  S 12 sts **M** 13 sts **L** 15 sts

- Knit across sock B heel stitches to marker, slip marker, work left side of sock B heel. Along right side of sock A heel, pick up and knit
  S 12 sts **M** 13 sts **L** 15 sts

Continue as established to the marker at the center of sock B heel.

Working the Gusset Decreases

Round 1

- On sock B heel, work to last 3 stitches, K2tog, K1.

- On sock A heel, K1, ssk, knit to last 3 stitches, K2tog, K1.

- Work instep stitches in H Sock Stitch on both socks as established. (Don't decrease on the instep stitches.)

- On sock B heel, K1, ssk, knit to marker. You have completed the first round of gusset decreases.

Round 2 Work even on all stitches.

Next Rounds Repeat Rounds 1 and 2 until each sock contains

S 48 sts   **M** 54 sts   **L** 60 sts

Working the Sock Feet

Continue on these stitches as established, working no further decreases, until the measurement from the back of the heel is

S 7 ″   **M** 7½″   **L** 8″
(17.75 cm)   (19 cm)   (20.25 cm)

or 1½″ (3.75 cm) less than the length of the foot of the intended wearer.

Decreasing for the Toes

Set Up Work one more round, ending at the beginning of sock B sole. Move the marker from the center of sock B sole to the beginning of sock B sole, to mark the new beginning of rounds.

Round 1

- On sock B sole, K1, ssk, knit to last 3 stitches, K2tog, K1.
- On sock A sole, K1, ssk, knit to last 3 stitches, K2tog, K1.
- On sock A instep, K1, ssk, knit to last 3 stitches, K2tog, K1.
- On sock B instep, K1, ssk, knit to last 3 stitches, K2tog, K1.

Round 2 Knit all stitches.

Next Rounds Repeat Rounds 1 and 2   **S** 5 more times   **M** 6 more times   **L** 7 more times

Next Rounds Repeat Round 1   **S** 4 more times   **M** 4 more times   **L** 5 more times

Each sock now has a total of   **S** 8 sts   **M** 10 sts   **L** 8 sts

Follow the Kitchener Stitch instructions on pages 28–29 to graft the toes closed.

Finishing

Weave in any loose ends. Block both socks, following the instructions on page 134.

H SOCK STITCH CHART

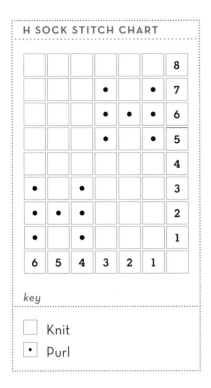

6	5	4	3	2	1	
						8
			•		•	7
			•	•	•	6
			•		•	5
						4
•		•				3
•	•	•				2
•		•				1

key

☐ Knit

• Purl

Athena

I love cables for their active strength. I am always amazed that simply moving stitches from here to there can create such amazing depth and character. This pattern is named for Athena, Greek goddess of war, handicraft, and wisdom: Bending, yet ultimately unyielding, power rests in these cables. The gentle twists among the more challenging cables bring a touch of femininity to the composition, completing an image of graceful stability.

YARN Louet Gems Merino Sport Weight, 100% merino wool, 3½ oz (100 g)/225 yds (206 m). Yarn band gauge: 5–6 stitches = 1″ (2.5 cm) in Stockinette Stitch on US 3–5 (3.25–3.75 mm needles.
Sage 50: **S** 1 skein; **M** 2 skeins; **L** 2 skeins

GAUGE 6 stitches and 8 rows = 1″ (2.5 cm) in Stockinette Stitch

NEEDLE US 4 (3.5 mm) 40″ (100 cm) circular, *or size needed to obtain correct gauge*

NOTIONS Stitch markers, tape measure, small cable needle, darning needle

SIZES **S** Women's Small
M Women's Medium
L Women's Large

FINISHED FOOT CIRCUMFERENCE
S 8½″ (21.5 cm)
M 9¼″ (23.5 cm)
L 10″ (25.5 cm)

Pattern Stitches

STOCKINETTE STITCH
Knit every round.

Knitting the Legs

Set Up For each sock, cast on **S** 52 sts **M** 56 sts **L** 60 sts

Note If desired, attach locking stitch marker or scrap of contrasting color yarn one stitch past join on sock A to mark the beginning of your work.

Work in K1, P1 rib for 2″ (5 cm).

Work the Athena Cable Pattern (page 103; two repeats of charted pattern equal one complete round of each sock). After working Lines 1–28 of Athena Cable Pattern once, repeat Lines 1–11 once more.

Leg measurement from cast-on edge is now about 6″ (15.25 cm).

Note End ready to begin sock A heel. Remove any markers used to denote beginning of round, and reserve for later.

Working the Heel Flaps

Note Work the heel flaps for both socks in rows at the same time on **S** 26 sts **M** 28 sts **L** 30 sts

Row 1 *Slip 1 stitch with yarn in back, K1; repeat from * to end of row.

Row 2 Slip the first stitch; purl to the end of row. (Note that the first heel flap row for sock B is Row 2.)

Next Rows Repeat Rows 1 and 2 **S** 12 more times **M** 13 more times **L** 14 more times

End having just worked Row 2.

The heel flaps now measure about **S** 2″ (5 cm) **M** 2½″ (6.25 cm) **L** 2¾″ (7 cm)

Turning the Heels

Note Turn the heel on each sock separately, beginning with sock A.

Row 1

 ▪ Knit across first **S** 15 sts **M** 16 sts **L** 17 sts

 ▪ Ssk, K1, turn.

Row 2 Slip 1, P5, P2tog, P1, turn.

Row 3 Slip 1, knit to one stitch before gap, ssk to close gap, K1, turn.

Row 4 Slip 1, purl to one stitch before gap, P2tog to close gap, P1, turn.

Next Rows Repeat Rows 3 and 4 until all stitches have been worked.

Sock A heel now has   **S** 15 sts   **M** 16 sts   **L** 17 sts

Follow directions above to turn sock B heel.

Picking Up Stitches for Gussets

Note Begin by picking up stitches on sock B heel.

Pick-Up Round

- Knit across sock B heel. Place a marker at the center of sock B heel. This represents the new beginning of rounds. With right side facing, along the left side of sock B heel pick up and knit
    S 13 sts   **M** 14 sts   **L** 15 sts

- Move to sock A, and knit across the heel stitches.

- Along left side of sock A heel, pick up and knit
    S 13 sts   **M** 14 sts   **L** 15 sts

- Work Athena Cable Pattern as established across sock A and B instep stitches.

- Along right side of sock B heel, pick up and knit
    S 13 sts   **M** 14 sts   **L** 15 sts

- Knit across sock B heel stitches to marker, slip marker, work left side of sock B heel. Along right side of sock A heel, pick up and knit
    S 13 sts   **M** 14 sts   **L** 15 sts

- Continue as established to the marker at the center of sock B heel.

Working the Gusset Decreases

Round 1

- On sock B heel, work to last 3 stitches, K2tog, K1.

- On sock A heel, K1, ssk, knit to last 3 stitches, K2tog, K1.

- Knit instep stitches in Athena Cable Pattern as established on both socks. (Don't decrease on the instep stitches.)

- On sock B heel, K1, ssk, knit to marker. You have completed the first round of gusset decreases.

Round 2 Work even on all stitches.

Next Rounds Repeat Rounds 1 and 2 until each sock contains
S 52 sts   **M** 56 sts   **L** 60 sts

Working the Sock Feet

Continue on these stitches as established, working no further decreases, until the measurement from the back of the heel is

S 7″   **M** 7¾″   **L** 8″
(17.75 cm)   (19.75 cm)   (20.25 cm)

or 1½″ (3.75 cm) less than the length of the foot of the intended wearer.

Decreasing for the Toes

Set Up Work one more round, ending at the beginning of sock B sole. Move the marker from the center of sock B sole to the beginning of sock B sole, to mark the new beginning of rounds.

Round 1

- On sock B sole, K1, ssk, knit to last 3 stitches, K2tog, K1.
- On sock A sole, K1, ssk, knit to last 3 stitches, K2tog, K1.
- On sock A instep, K1, ssk, knit to last 3 stitches, K2tog, K1.
- On sock B instep, K1, ssk, knit to last 3 stitches, K2tog, K1.

Round 2 Knit all stitches.

Next Rounds Work Rounds 1 and 2
S 5 more times   **M** 6 more times   **L** 7 more times

Next Rounds Work Round 1
S 5 more times   **M** 5 more times   **L** 5 more times

Each sock now has a total of 8 stitches: 4 instep and 4 sole stitches.

Follow the Kitchener Stitch instructions on pages 28–29 to graft the toes closed.

Finishing

Weave in any loose ends. Block both socks, following the instructions on page 134.

ATHENA CABLE PATTERN

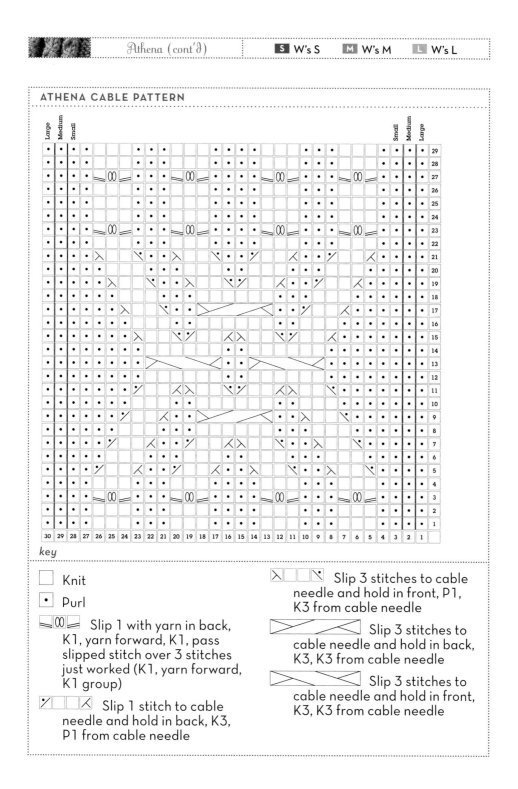

key

	Knit
•	Purl

Slip 1 with yarn in back, K1, yarn forward, K1, pass slipped stitch over 3 stitches just worked (K1, yarn forward, K1 group)

Slip 1 stitch to cable needle and hold in back, K3, P1 from cable needle

Slip 3 stitches to cable needle and hold in front, P1, K3 from cable needle

Slip 3 stitches to cable needle and hold in back, K3, K3 from cable needle

Slip 3 stitches to cable needle and hold in front, K3, K3 from cable needle

Emily's Socks

A few years ago, my best friend's daughter, little Emily Jane, preempted everyone's plans by coming a month early. She was tiny, with the translucent skin of a baby born a bit too soon. And she had the littlest feet. I measured them the day she was born and began knitting socks for her immediately. Looking just like her dad and sharing her mother's spirit, she didn't just "do well," she positively blossomed. A year later, it was clear that this adorable little girl was right on time.

YARN   Schaefer Anne, 60% superwash merino wool/25% mohair/15% nylon, fingering weight, 4 oz (113 g)/560 yds (512 m). Yarn band gauge: 7 stitches = 1" (2.5 cm) in Stockinette Stitch on US 1 (2.5 mm) needles. 1 skein

GAUGE   8 stitches and 10 rows = 1" (2.5 cm)

NEEDLE   US 1 (2.5 mm) 40" (100 cm) circular, *or size needed to obtain correct gauge*

NOTIONS   Stitch markers, tape measure, darning needle

SIZES
- **S** Child's Small: 2–4
- **M** Child's Medium: 6–8
- **L** Child's Large: 10–12

FINISHED FOOT CIRCUMFERENCE
- **S** 4" (10 cm)
- **M** 5" (12.75 cm)
- **L** 7" (17.75 cm)

Pattern Stitches

RIBBING
K1, P1.

STOCKINETTE STITCH
Knit every round.

EMILY STITCH PATTERN
ROUNDS 1, 3, AND 4 Knit all stitches.
ROUND 2 *K3tog, leaving these three stitches on the left-hand needle. Knit into the first stitch, then knit the second and third stitches together, creating three stitches from the K3tog bundle; repeat from * to end of round.

Knitting the Legs

Set Up For each sock, cast on **S** 36 sts **M** 48 sts **L** 60 sts

Note If desired, attach locking stitch marker or scrap of contrasting color yarn one stitch past join on sock A to mark the beginning of your work.

For Ribbing Top (photo, pg. 105)

Work in K2, P2 ribbing for 1½″ (3.75 cm).

For Picot Edging Top (cover photo)

Rounds 1–5 Knit.

Round 6 *Work Picot Edge Stitch:* *K2tog, YO; repeat from * around both socks.

Rounds 7–11 Knit.

Round 12 *Turn picot edge:* Knit one live stitch on needle together with back loop of first cast-on stitch. This joins the two together and creates a finished and turned hem edge for the sock. Knit each successive live stitch together with its cast-on counterpart until the hems on both socks are completed.

For Both Tops

Work in Emily Stitch Pattern (see page 109) until leg measures

 S 4 ″ **M** 5 ″ **L** 6 ″
 (10 cm) (12.75 cm) (15.25 cm)

Note End ready to begin sock A heel. Remove any markers used to denote beginning of round, and reserve for later.

Working the Heel Flaps

Note Work heel flaps for both socks in rows at the same time, on

 S 18 sts **M** 24 sts **L** 30 sts

Row 1 *Slip 1 stitch with yarn in back, K1; repeat from * to end of row.

Row 2 Slip the first stitch, purl to end of row. (Note that the first heel flap row for sock B is Row 2.)

Next Rows Repeat Rows 1 and 2

 S 7 **M** 8 **L** 9
 more more more
 times times times

End having just worked Row 2.

The heel flaps now measure about

 S 1 ″ **M** 1½″ **L** 1¾″
 (2.5 cm) (3.75 cm) (4.5 cm)

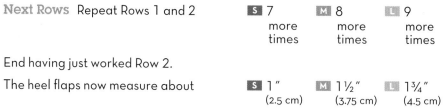

Turning the Heels

Note Turn the heel on each sock separately, beginning with sock A.

Row 1

- Knit across first   **S** 11 sts   **M** 14 sts   **L** 17 sts
- Ssk, K1, turn.

Row 2 Slip 1, P5, P2tog, P1, turn.

Row 3 Slip 1, knit to one stitch before gap, ssk to close gap, K1, turn.

Row 4 Slip 1, purl to one stitch before gap, P2tog to close gap, P1, turn.

Next Rows Repeat Rows 3 and 4 until all stitches have been worked.

Sock A heel now has   **S** 11 sts   **M** 14 sts   **L** 17 sts

Follow directions above to turn sock B heel.

Picking Up Stitches for Gussets

Note Begin by picking up the stitches on sock B heel.

Pick-Up Round

- Knit across sock B heel. Place a marker at the center of sock B heel. This represents the new beginning of rounds. With right side facing and working along the left side, pick up and knit
  S 8 sts   **M** 9 sts   **L** 10 sts
- Move to sock A, and knit across the heel stitches.
- Along left side of heel flap A, pick up and knit
  S 8 sts   **M** 9 sts   **L** 10 sts
- Work across sock A and B instep stitches in Emily Stitch Pattern as established.
- Along right side of sock B heel, pick up and knit
  S 8 sts   **M** 9 sts   **L** 10 sts
- Knit across sock B heel stitches to marker, slide marker, work left side of sock B heel. Along right side of sock A heel, pick up and knit
  S 8 sts   **M** 9 sts   **L** 10 sts
- Continue as established to the marker at the center of sock B heel.

Working the Gusset Decreases

Round 1

- On sock B heel, work to last 3 stitches, K2tog, K1.
- On sock A heel, K1, ssk, knit to last 3 stitches, K2tog, K1.
- Work instep stitches in Emily Stitch Pattern as established on both socks. (Don't decrease on instep stitches.)
- On sock B heel, knit 1, ssk, knit to marker. You have completed the first round of gusset decreases.

Round 2   Work even on all stitches.

Next Rounds   Repeat Rounds 1 and 2 until each sock contains

S 36 sts   **M** 48 sts   **L** 60 sts

Working the Sock Feet

Continue on these stitches as established, working no further decreases, until the measurement from the back of the heel is

S 3″   **M** 4½″   **L** 6″
(7.5 cm)   (11.5 cm)   (15.25 cm)

or 1½″ less than the length of the foot of the intended wearer.

Decreasing for the Toes

Set Up   Work one more round, ending at the beginning of sock B sole. Move the marker from the center of sock B sole to the beginning of sock B sole, to mark the new beginning of rounds.

Round 1

- On sock B sole, K1, ssk, knit to last 3 stitches, K2tog, K1.
- On sock A sole, K1, ssk, knit to last 3 stitches, K2tog, K1.
- On sock A instep, K1, ssk, knit to last 3 stitches, K2tog, K1.
- On sock B instep, K1, ssk , knit to last 3 stitches, K2tog, K1.

Round 2   Knit all stitches.

Next Rounds   Work alternating decrease and even rounds

S 3   **M** 5   **L** 5
more   more   more
times   times   times

		S	**M**	**L**
Next Rounds	Repeat Round 1	3 more times	4 more times	5 more times
Each sock has a total of		8 sts	8 sts	16 sts
including soles and insteps each with		4 sts	4 sts	8 sts

Follow the Kitchener Stitch instructions on pages 28–29 to graft the toes closed.

Finishing

Weave in any loose ends. Block both socks, following the instructions on page 134.

EMILY STITCH PATTERN

			4
			3
✕ (spanning)			2
			1
3	2	1	

key

☐ Knit

✕ Knit 3 together, leaving all 3 stitches on left needle, knit into first stitch, knit 2 together

Sailor's Delight

I love this pattern, and the way the yarn-over eyelets ripple down the sock leg reminds me of waves on deep Pacific waters. Knit in rich blues and greens, its effect is even more aquatic. This lace pattern is a good one to tackle once you've finished a few pairs of socks; you can float along with the familiar rhythm of sock construction as you stay mindful of the moving stitch pattern.

YARN Schaefer Anne, 60% superwash merino wool/25% mohair/15% nylon, fingering weight, 4 oz (113 g)/560 yds (512 m). Yarn band gauge: 7 stitches = 1" (2.5 cm) in Stockinette Stitch on US 1 (2.5 mm) needles. 1 skein

GAUGE 8 stitches and 10 rows = 1" (2.5 cm) in Stockinette Stitch

NEEDLE US 1 (2.5 mm) 40" (100 cm) circular, *or size needed to obtain correct gauge*

NOTIONS stitch markers, tape measure, darning needle

SIZES
- **S** Women's Small
- **M** Women's Medium
- **L** Women's Large

FINISHED FOOT CIRCUMFERENCE
- **S** 8" (20.25 cm)
- **M** 9" (22.75 cm)
- **L** 10" (25.5 cm)

Pattern Stitches

RIBBING
K1, P1

STOCKINETTE STITCH
Knit every round.

SAILOR'S DELIGHT STITCH PATTERN
ROUND 1 *K1, K2tog, K2, yo, K1; repeat from * around.
ROUNDS 2 AND 4 Knit.
ROUND 3 *K2tog, K2, yo, K2; repeat from * around.

Knitting the Legs

Set Up For each sock, cast on · **S** 60 sts · **M** 72 sts · **L** 84 sts

Note If desired, attach locking stitch marker or scrap of contrasting color yarn one stitch past join on sock A to mark the beginning of your work.

Work in K1, P1 rib for 2″ (5 cm).

Work the Sailor's Delight Stitch Pattern (see page 115) until cuff measures

S 6½″ · **M** 7″ · **L** 7″
(16.5 cm) · (17.75 cm) · (17.75 cm)

Note End ready to begin sock A heel. Remove any markers used to denote beginning of round, and reserve for later.

Working the Heel Flaps

Note Work the heel flaps for both socks in rows at the same time on

S 30 sts · **M** 36 sts · **L** 42 sts

Row 1 *Slip 1 stitch with yarn in back, K1; repeat from * to end of row.

Row 2 Slip the first stitch, purl to end of row. (Note that the first heel flap row for sock B is Row 2.)

Next Rows Repeat Rows 1 and 2

S 15 more times · **M** 17 more times · **L** 18 more times

End having just worked Row 2.

The heel flaps now measure about

S 2″ · **M** 2¼″ · **L** 2½″
(5 cm) · (5.75 cm) · (6.25 cm)

Turning the Heels

Note Turn heels separately, working in rows and beginning with sock A.

Row 1
- Knit · **S** 17 sts · **M** 20 sts · **L** 23 sts
- Ssk, K1, turn.

Row 2 Slip 1, P5, P2tog, P1, turn.

Row 3 Slip 1, knit to one stitch before gap, ssk to close gap, K1, turn.

Row 4 Slip 1, purl to one stitch before gap, P2tog, P1, turn.

Next Rows Repeat Rows 3 and 4 until all stitches have been worked.

Sock A heel now has **S** 17 sts **M** 20 sts **L** 22 sts

Follow directions above to turn sock B heel.

Picking Up Stitches for Gussets

Note Begin by picking up stitches on sock B heel.

Pick-Up Round

- Knit across sock B heel. Place a marker at the center of sock B heel. This represents the new beginning of rounds. With right side facing, along the left side of sock B heel pick up and knit **S** 16 sts **M** 18 sts **L** 21 sts

- Move to sock A, and knit across the heel stitches.

- Along left side of sock A heel, pick up and knit **S** 16 sts **M** 18 sts **L** 21 sts

- Work Sailor's Delight Stitch Pattern as established across sock A and B instep stitches.

- Along right side of sock B heel, pick up and knit **S** 16 sts **M** 18 sts **L** 21 sts

- Knit across sock B heel stitches to marker, slip marker, work left side of sock B heel. Along right side of sock A heel, pick up and knit **S** 16 sts **M** 18 sts **L** 21 sts

- Continue as established to the marker at the center of sock B heel.

Working the Gusset Decreases

Round 1

- On sock B heel, work to last 3 stitches, K2tog, K1.

- On sock A heel, K1, ssk, knit to last 3 stitches, K2tog, K1.

- Knit instep stitches on both socks as established. (Don't decrease on the instep stitches.)

- On sock B heel, K1, ssk, knit to marker. You have completed the first round of gusset decreases.

Round 2 Work even on all stitches.

Next Rounds Repeat Rounds 1 and 2 until each sock contains

S 60 sts   **M** 72 sts   **L** 76 sts

Working the Sock Feet

Continue on these stitches as established, working no further decreases, until the measurement from the back of the heel is

S 7″   **M** 7½″   **L** 8″
(17.75 cm)   (19 cm)   (20.25 cm)

or 1½″ (3.75 cm) less than the length of the foot of the intended wearer.

Note Remove any markers used to denote beginning of round, and reserve for later.

Decreasing for the Toes

Set Up Work one more round, ending at the beginning of sock B sole. Move the marker from the center of sock B sole to the beginning of sock B sole, to mark the new beginning of rounds.

Round 1

- On sock B sole, K1, ssk, knit to last 3 stitches, K2tog, K1.
- On sock A sole, K1, ssk, knit to last 3 stitches, K2tog, K1.
- On sock A instep, K1, ssk, knit to last 3 stitches, K2tog, K1.
- On sock B instep, K1, ssk, knit to last 3 stitches, K2tog, K1.

Round 2 Knit all stitches.

Next Rounds Repeat Rounds 1 and 2   **S** 5 more times   **M** 7 more times   **L** 7 more times

Next Rounds

- Repeat Round 1   **S** 5 more times   **M** 6 more times   **L** 7 more times

Each sock now has a total of 16 stitches: 8 instep and 8 sole stitches.

Follow the Kitchener Stitch instructions on pages 28–29 to graft the toes closed.

Finishing

Weave in any loose ends. Block both socks, following the instructions on page 134.

SAILOR'S DELIGHT STITCH PATTERN

6	5	4	3	2	1	
						4
		o			/	3
						2
	o			/		1

key

☐ Knit

◻ Knit 2 together

o Yarn over

Pitter Patter

This is, among other things, an excellent first sock. The very simple ribbed cuff and stockinette-stitch leg allow a novice sock knitter to focus on sock anatomy and technique. I often advise folks learning a new technique to start with a child-sized item; smaller sizes mean less knitting time and less time lost for errors. I know I'd rather have my learning experiences on something small, and kids are not likely to notice missed, twisted, or reknit stitches!

YARN Valley Yarns Superwash, 100% extra-fine merino wool, worsted weight, 1½ oz (50gm)/97yds (88 m). Yarn band gauge: 4½ stitches = 1″ (2.5 cm) in Stockinette Stitch on US 8 (5 mm) needles. Colonial Blue 501: **S** 1 skein; **M** 2 skeins; **L** 2 skeins

GAUGE 5½ stitches and 7½ rows = 1″ (2.5 cm) in Stockinette Stitch

NEEDLE US 4 (3.5 mm) 40″ (100 cm) circular, *or size needed to obtain correct gauge*

NOTIONS Stitch markers, tape measure, darning needle

SIZES **S** Child's Small: 2–4
M Child's Medium: 6–8
L Child's Large: 10–12

FINISHED FOOT CIRCUMFERENCE
S 5″ (12.75 cm)
M 6″ (15.25 cm)
L 7″ (17.75 cm)

Pattern Stitches

RIBBING
K1, P1.

STOCKINETTE STITCH
Knit every round.

Knitting the Legs

Set Up For each sock, cast on **S** 28 sts **M** 32 sts **L** 40 sts

Note If desired, attach locking stitch marker or scrap of contrasting color yarn to your work one stitch over from your join on sock A to mark the beginning of your work.

Work in K1, P1 ribbing until cuff measurement is

S 1″ **M** 1½″ **L** 1¾″
(2.5 cm) (3.75 cm) (4.5 cm)

Work in Stockinette Stitch until sock measurement from cast-on edge is

S 4″ **M** 5″ **L** 6″
(10 cm) (12.75 cm) (15.25 cm)

Note End ready to begin sock A heel. Remove any markers used to denote beginning of round, and reserve for later.

Working the Heel Flaps

Note Work the heel flaps for both socks in rows at the same time on

S 14 sts **M** 16 sts **L** 20 sts

Row 1 *Slip 1 stitch with yarn in back, K1; repeat from * to end of row.

Row 2 Slip the first stitch; purl to the end of row. (Note that the first heel flap row for sock B is Row 2.)

Next Rows Repeat Rows 1 and 2

S 13 **M** 15 **L** 17
more more more
times times times

End having just worked Row 2.

The heel flaps now measure about

S 1″ **M** 1½″ **L** 1¾″
(2.5 cm) (3.75 cm) (4.5 cm)

Turning the Heels

Note Turn the heel on each sock separately, beginning with sock A.

Row 1

- Knit across first **S** 9 sts **M** 10 sts **L** 12 sts
- Ssk, K1, turn.

Row 2 Slip 1, P5, P2tog, P1, turn.

Row 3 Slip 1, knit to one stitch before gap, ssk to close gap, K1, turn.

Row 4 Slip 1, purl to one stitch before gap, P2tog to close gap, P1, turn.

Next Rows Repeat Rows 3 and 4 until all stitches have been worked.

Sock A heel now has   **S** 10 sts   **M** 10 sts   **L** 12 sts

Follow directions above to turn sock B heel.

Picking Up Stitches for Gussets

Note Begin by picking up stitches on sock B heel.

Pick-Up Round

- Knit across sock B heel. Place a marker at the center of sock B heel. This represents the new beginning of rounds. With right side facing, along the left side of heel flap B pick up and knit

    S 7 sts   **M** 8 sts   **L** 9 sts

- Move to sock A, and knit across the heel stitches.

- Along left side of sock A heel, pick up and knit

    S 7 sts   **M** 8 sts   **L** 9 sts

- Work across sock A and B instep stitches.

- Along right side of sock B heel, pick up and knit

    S 7 sts   **M** 8 sts   **L** 9 sts

- Knit across sock B heel stitches to marker, slip marker, work left side of sock B heel. On right side of sock A heel, pick up and knit

    S 7 sts   **M** 8 sts   **L** 9 sts

- Continue as established to the marker at the center of sock B heel.

Working the Gusset Decreases

Round 1

- On sock B heel, work to last 3 stitches, K2tog, K1.
- On sock A heel, K1, ssk, knit to last 3 stitches, K2tog, K1.
- Knit instep stitches on both socks. (Don't decrease on the instep stitches.)
- On sock B heel, K1, ssk, knit to marker. You have completed the first round of gusset decreases.

Round 2 Work even on all stitches.

Next Rounds Repeat Rounds 1 and 2 until each sock contains

S 28 sts   **M** 32 sts   **L** 40 sts

Working the Sock Feet

Continue on these stitches as established, working no further decreases, until the measurement from the back of the heel is

S 2½"   **M** 4"   **L** 5"
(7.5 cm)   (10 cm)   (12.75 cm)

or 1½" (3.75 cm) less than the length of the foot of the intended wearer.

Decreasing for the Toes

Set Up Work one more round, ending at the beginning of sock B sole. Move the marker from the center of sock B sole to the beginning of sock B sole, to mark the new beginning of rounds.

Round 1

- On sock B sole, K1, ssk, knit to last 3 stitches, K2tog, K1.
- On sock A sole, K1, ssk, knit to last 3 stitches, K2tog, K1.
- On sock A instep, K1, ssk, knit to last 3 stitches, K2tog, K1.
- On sock B instep, K1, ssk, knit to last 3 stitches, K2tog, K1.

Round 2 Knit all stitches even.

Next Rounds Knit Rounds 1 and 2   **S** 4   **M** 5   **L** 7
more   more   more
times   times   times

Each sock now a total of 8 stitches: 4 instep and 4 sole stitches.

Follow the Kitchener Stitch instructions on pages 28–29 to graft the toes closed.

Finishing

Weave in any loose ends. Block both socks, following the instructions on page 134.

The Classic Sock

Simple, basic, and to the point. No furbelows, fluff, or nonsense. Many sock recipients, especially men, prefer a simple sock. For this kind of knitting, an intriguing yarn is crucial for keeping the knitter's attention. A yarn with smooth color changes will hold the knitter's interest yet remain subtle enough for the pickiest guy. This traditional sock is also simple to knit, making it an excellent project for beginners.

YARN Zitron Trekking XXL, 75% superwash wool/25% nylon, fingering weight, 3½"oz (100 g)/459 yds (420 m). Yarn band gauge: 7–8 stitches = 1" (2.5 cm) on US 0–2 (2–3 mm) needles.
Color 69: 1 skein

GAUGE 9½ stitches and 11 rows = 1" (2.5 cm) in Stockinette Stitch

NEEDLE US 1 (2.25 mm) 40" (100 cm) circular, or *size needed to obtain correct gauge*

NOTIONS stitch markers, tape measure, darning needle

SIZES LS Women's Large/Men's Small
M Men's Medium
L Men's Large

FINISHED FOOT CIRCUMFERENCE
LS 8½" (21.5 cm)
M 9" (22.75 cm)
L 10"(25.5 cm)

Pattern Stitches

RIBBING A
K1, P1.

RIBBING B
K3, P1.

STOCKINETTE STITCH
Knit every round.

Knitting the Legs

Set Up For each sock, cast on   **L S** 80 sts   **M** 88 sts   **L** 96 sts

Note If desired, attach locking stitch marker or scrap of contrasting color yarn to your work one stitch over from your join on sock A to mark the beginning of your work.

Work in K1, P1 ribbing until measurement from cast-on edge is 2″ (5 cm).

Work in K3, P1 ribbing until leg measurement from cast-on edge is 9" (22.5 cm).

Note End ready to begin sock A heel. Remove any markers used to denote beginning of round, and reserve for later.

Working the Heel Flaps

Note Work the heel flaps for both socks in rows at the same time on   **L S** 40 sts   **M** 44 sts   **L** 48 sts

Row 1 *Slip 1 stitch with yarn in back, K1; repeat from * to end of row.

Row 2 Slip the first stitch; purl to the end of row. (Note that the first heel flap row for sock B is Row 2.)

Next Rows Repeat Rows 1 and 2   **L S** 21 more times   **M** 23 more times   **L** 25 more times

End having just worked Row 2.

The heel flaps now measure about   **L S** 2″ (5 cm)   **M** 2¼″ (5.75 cm)   **L** 2½″ (6.25 cm)

Turning the Heels

Note Turn the heel on each sock separately, beginning with sock A.

Row 1

- Knit across first   **L S** 22 sts   **M** 24 sts   **L** 26 sts
- Ssk, K1, turn.

Row 2 Slip 1, P5, P2tog, P1, turn.

Row 3 Slip 1, knit to one stitch before gap, ssk to close gap, K1, turn.

Row 4 Slip 1, purl to one stitch before gap, P2tog to close gap, P1, turn.

Next Rows Repeat Rows 3 and 4 until all stitches have been worked.

Sock A heel now has   **L S** 22 sts   **M** 24 sts   **L** 26 sts

Follow directions above to turn sock B heel.

Picking Up Stitches for Gussets

Note Begin by picking up stitches on sock B heel.

Pick-Up Round

- Knit across sock B heel. Place a marker at the center of sock B heel. This represents the new beginning of rounds. With right side facing, along the left side of sock B heel pick up and knit

  L S 22 sts   **M** 24 sts   **L** 26 sts
- Move to sock A, and knit across the heel stitches.
- Along left side of sock A heel, pick up and knit

  L S 22 sts   **M** 24 sts   **L** 26 sts
- Work in K3, P1 ribbing as established across sock A and B instep stitches.
- Along right side of sock B heel, pick up and knit

  L S 22 sts   **M** 24 sts   **L** 26 sts
- Knit across sock B heel stitches to marker, slip marker, work left side of sock B heel. Along right side of sock A heel, pick up and knit

  L S 22 sts   **M** 24 sts   **L** 26 sts
- Continue as established to the marker at the center of sock B heel.

Working the Gusset Decreases

Round 1

- On sock B heel, work to last 3 stitches, K2tog, K1.
- On sock A heel, K1, ssk, knit to last 3 stitches, K2tog, K1.
- Knit instep stitches in K3, P1 ribbing as established on both socks. (Don't decrease on the instep stitches.)
- On sock B heel, K1, ssk, knit to marker. You have completed the first round of gusset decreases.

Round 2 Work even on all stitches.

Next Rounds Repeat Rounds 1 and 2 until each sock contains

     S 80 sts   **M** 88 sts   **L** 96 sts

Working the Sock Feet

Continue on these stitches as established, working no further decreases, until the measurement from the back of the heel is

     S 8"   **M** 9"   **L** 9¾"
     (20.25 cm)   (22.75 cm)   (24.75 cm)

or 1½" (3.75 cm) less than the length of the foot of the intended wearer.

Decreasing for the Toes

Set Up Work one more round, ending at the beginning of sock B sole. Move the marker from the center of sock B sole to the beginning of sock B sole, to mark the new beginning of rounds.

Round 1

- On sock B sole, K1, ssk, knit to last 3 stitches, K2tog, K1.
- On sock A sole, K1, ssk, knit to last 3 stitches, K2tog, K1.
- On sock A instep, K1, ssk, knit to last 3 stitches, K2tog, K1.
- On sock B instep, K1, ssk, knit to last 3 stitches, K2tog, K1.

Round 2 Knit all stitches even.

Next Rounds Knit Rounds 1 and 2   **S** 8 more times   **M** 9 more times   **L** 10 more times

Next Rounds Knit Round 1   **S** 7 more times   **M** 8 more times   **L** 9 more times

Each sock now has a total of 16 stitches: 8 instep and 8 sole stitches.

Follow the Kitchener Stitch instructions on pages 28–29 to graft the toes closed.

Finishing

Weave in any loose ends. Block both socks, following the instructions on page 134.

Ragg Hiker

These are almost exactly like my favorite ragg hiking socks — simple to knit, comfortable to wear. Knitted in any worsted-weight yarn, they are wonderfully thick socks, perfect for fall hikes or mountain-bike rides. Soft wool ensures warmth and comfort. The simple rib makes these a great beginner sock, and for those who thrive on instant gratification, the gauge means a little less time at the needles.

YARN	Louet Gems Merino Light Worsted, 100% merino wool, 3½ oz (100g)/175 yds (160 m). Yarn band gauge: 4½–5 stitches = 1" (2.5 cm) on US 5–7 (3.75–4.5 mm) needles. Black Eyed Susan 88 or Peony 80: 2 skeins
GAUGE	6 stitches and 8 rows = 1" (2.5 cm) in Stockinette Stitch
NEEDLE	US 3 (3.25 mm) 40" (100 cm) circular, or size needed to obtain correct gauge
NOTIONS	Stitch markers, tape measure, darning needle
SIZES	M Women's Medium
	LS Women's Large/Men's Small
	M Men's Medium

FINISHED FOOT CIRCUMFERENCE
- M 8½" (21.5 cm)
- LS 9¼" (23.5 cm)
- M 10" (25.5 cm)

Pattern Stitches

RIBBING
K2, P2.

STOCKINETTE STITCH
Knit every row.

Knitting the Legs

Set Up For each sock, cast on　　**M** 52 sts　**LS** 56 sts　**M** 60 sts

Note If desired, attach locking stitch marker or scrap of contrasting color yarn one stitch past join on sock A to mark the beginning of your work.

Work in K2, P2 ribbing until leg measures

M 7"　　　　**LS** 8"　　　　**M** 9"
(17.75 cm)　　(20.25 cm)　　(22.75 cm)

Note End ready to begin sock A heel. Remove any markers used to denote beginning of round, and reserve for later.

Working the Heel Flaps

Note Work the heel flaps for both socks in rows at the same time on

M 26 sts　**LS** 28 sts　**M** 30 sts

Row 1 *Slip 1 stitch with yarn in back, K1; repeat from * to end of row.

Row 2 Slip the first stitch, purl to end of row. (Note that the first heel flap row for sock B is Row 2.)

Next Rows Repeat Rows 1 and 2

M 12 more times	**LS** 13 more times	**M** 14 more times

End having just worked Row 2.

The heel flaps now measure about

M 2"　　　**LS** 2¼"　　　**M** 2½"
(5 cm)　　(5.75 cm)　　(6.25 cm)

Turning the Heels

Note Turn the heel on each sock separately, beginning with sock A.

Row 1

- Knit across first　　**M** 15 sts　**LS** 16 sts　**M** 17 sts

- Ssk, K1, turn.

Row 2 Slip 1, P5, P2tog, P1, turn.

Row 3 Slip 1, knit to one stitch before gap, ssk to close gap, K1, turn.

Row 4 Slip 1, purl to one stitch before gap, P2tog to close gap, P1, turn.

Next Rows Repeat Rows 3 and 4 until all stitches have been worked.

Sock A heel now has   **M** 16 sts   **LS** 16 sts   **M** 17 sts

Follow directions above to turn sock B heel.

Picking Up Stitches for Gussets

Note   Begin by picking up stitches on sock B heel.

Pick-Up Round

- Knit across sock B heel. Place a marker at the center of sock B heel. This represents the new beginning of rounds. With right side facing, along the left side of sock B heel pick up and knit

  M 13 st   **LS** 14 sts   **M** 15 sts

- Move to sock A, and knit across the heel stitches.
- Along left side of sock A heel, pick up and knit

  M 13 sts   **LS** 14 sts   **M** 15 sts

- Work across sock A and B instep stitches in K2, P2 ribbing as established.
- Along right side of sock B heel, pick up and knit

  M 13 sts   **LS** 14 sts   **M** 15 sts

- Knit across sock B heel stitches to marker, slip marker, work left side of sock B heel. Along right side of sock A heel, pick up and knit

  M 13 sts   **LS** 14 sts   **M** 15 sts

- Continue as established to the marker at the center of sock B heel.

Working the Gusset Decreases

Round 1

- On sock B heel, work to last 3 stitches, K2tog, K1.
- On sock A heel, K1, ssk, knit to last 3 stitches, K2tog, K1.
- Knit instep stitches on both socks as established. (Don't decrease on the instep stitches.)
- On sock B heel, K1, ssk, knit to marker. You have completed the first round of gusset decreases.

Round 2   Work even on all stitches.

Next Rounds   Repeat Rounds 1 and 2 until each sock contains

     M 52 sts   **LS** 56 sts   **M** 60 sts

Working the Sock Feet

Continue on these stitches as established, working no further decreases, until the measurement from the back of the heel is

M 7¾"   **LS** 8"   **M** 9"
(19.75 cm)   (20.25 cm)   (22.75 cm)

or 1½" (3.75 cm) less than the length of the foot of the intended wearer.

Note Remove any markers used to denote beginning of round, and reserve for later use.

Decreasing for the Toes

Set Up Work one more round, ending at the beginning of sock B sole. Move the marker from the center of sock B sole to the beginning of sock B sole, to mark the new beginning of rounds.

Round 1

- On sock B sole, K1, ssk, knit to last 3 stitches, K2tog, K1.
- On sock A sole, K1, ssk, knit to last 3 stitches, K2tog, K1.
- On sock A instep, K1, ssk, knit to last 3 stitches, K2tog, K1.
- On sock B instep, K1, ssk, knit to last 3 stitches, K2tog, K1.

Round 2 Knit all stitches even.

Next Rounds Repeat Rounds 1 and 2   **M** 5 more times   **LS** 6 more times   **M** 7 more times

Next Rounds Repeat Round 1   **M** 5 more times   **LS** 5 more times   **M** 5 more times

Each sock now has a total of 8 stitches: 4 instep and 4 sole stitches.

Follow the Kitchener Stitch instructions on pages 28–29 to graft toe closed.

Finishing

Weave in any loose ends. Block both socks, following the instructions on page 134.

APPENDIX

Glossary

Decreases

SLIP, SLIP, KNIT (ssk)

Slip two stitches, one at a time as if to knit, from the left-hand needle to the right-hand needle. Insert left-hand needle into the two slipped stitches through the front loops, and knit them together.

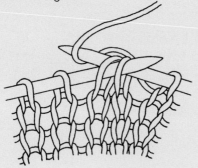

KNIT TWO TOGETHER (K2tog)

Insert right-hand needle into the next two stitches on the left-hand needle through the front loops, and knit them together.

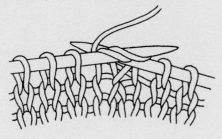

PURL TWO TOGETHER (P2tog)

Insert the right-hand needle into the next two stitches on the left-hand needle through the front loops and purl them together.

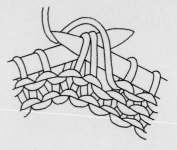

Increases

KNIT IN THE FRONT AND BACK OF THE STITCH (KIF&B)

Insert the right-hand needle into the next stitch on your left-hand needle and knit it as usual. Do not remove the stitch from the needle. Insert the right-hand needle into the back of the stitch just worked, and knit it a second time. Move to right-hand needle.

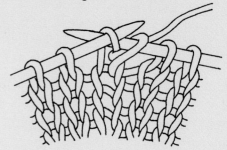

YARN OVER (yo)

Bring the working yarn to the front between the two needles. Bring the working yarn over the right-hand needle to the back before you make your next knit stitch.

Other Techniques and Terms

LONG-TAIL CAST-ON

Sometimes called the *slingshot cast-on*, this one is among the most used and arguably the most versatile. It creates a flexible edge that is perfect for most garments. Make a slipknot and place it on a needle, leaving a very long tail. Hold the needle in your right hand.

Grasp both yarns in your left hand in a fist. Slide your index finger and thumb between the two yarns and open your fingers in an "L" shape.

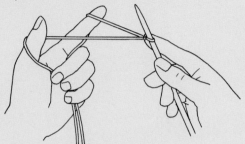

index and thumb in place to begin cast on

Turn your hand so that you are looking at your palm. Slide the needle in your right hand up and through the loop of yarn on your thumb.

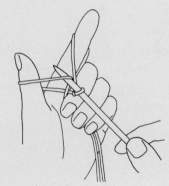

sliding needle under thumb yarn

How Long Is Your Long Tail?

To determine how much yarn you need for the tail, wrap your yarn loosely around your needle once for each stitch you'll cast on. Make your slipknot, then slide the wrapped yarn off the needle and use it for your cast-on tail.

Catch the yarn on your index finger and bring it back through the loop on your thumb.

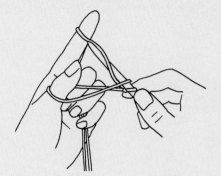

catching the yarn on the index finger

Pull both yarns snugly, but not tightly. Continue until you've cast on the correct number of stitches.

stitch cast on mounted correctly

BLOCKING

Most of the time when I complete a pair of socks, they move off the needles and onto my family's feet without a moment's thought. For gift-giving, however, I block. To block finished socks, first soak them in warm water and a no-rinse wool wash such as Eucalan. Squeeze them to remove excess water. Place them in an empty washing machine and run one *spin only* cycle. A great low-cost, low-energy alternative to this is a salad spinner; I like OXO's

large-capacity model. Once you've spun the socks, remove them from the washing machine or spinner and place them on sock blockers to dry. Fiber Trends offers these in a variety of sizes, but you can also make your own out of old wire coat hangers bent into the shape and size of a foot. Allow the socks to dry completely before removing from the blocker.

GAUGE

Gauge, the number of stitches in an inch, determines how many stitches are used to create any knitted garment. All gauge references in these patterns are based on swatches knit at *least* 4 inches wide by 4 inches long in stockinette stitch. If your swatch does not yield the gauge recommended for a pattern, change your needle size and swatch again. If, for example, a sock pattern calls for a gauge of 6 stitches per inch, on size 4 US (3.5 mm) needles, and you are knitting at 6.5 stitches per inch on that needle size, try again on a larger needle, in this case, size 5 (3.75 mm). However, if you are getting fewer than 6 stitches in an inch, switch to a smaller needle (start with a size US 3 [3.25 mm]). *For best results, do not cast on for your socks until you've swatched at the correct gauge.* A good rule of thumb: Your gauge will change about one quarter to one half stitch per inch for every needle size change.

PICK UP AND KNIT

With the right side facing you, insert the right-hand needle into the next stitch or space at the edge of the row. Bring the working yarn over the needle and knit.

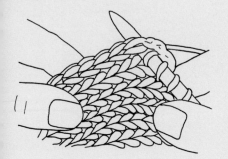

pick up and knit

STRANDING

To work with more than one color while knitting is not difficult, if you follow one key strategy: Do not carry your yarn for more than three stitches without twisting the colors on the wrong side of the work.

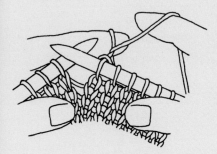

twisting yarn to prevent long floats

Carrying your yarn across too many stitches results in long floats that can catch fingers and toes and cause stitch distortion on the right side of your work.

WEAVING IN ENDS

When your project is complete, you will be left with tail ends. First take the tail ends to the wrong side of your fabric, threading them onto a darning needle to draw them through. Using the darning needle, weave each tail, one at a time, across the wrong side of the fabric, under the purl bumps of the stitches. A general rule of thumb is to weave each yarn end across a minimum of four stitches and change direction at least three times. Once you have woven in the yarn, use your fingers to gently tug and stretch the fabric a bit to even the tension, then clip the yarn end close to the work. On most woolen items, this yarn will not unravel. But for slippery fibers such as cotton, bamboo, or silk, make four directional changes, and possibly place a tiny dot of a solution such as Dritz Fray Check where you plan to cut the yarn tail. Allow the Fray Check to dry thoroughly and then clip close to the work surface.

Pattern Stitch Key

□ Knit

• Purl

○ Yarn over

V Slip as if to purl

\ Slip, slip, knit the slipped stitches together

/ Knit 2 together

/. Purl 2 together

⋏ Knit 3 together

M Make 1

M Purl into the front and back

U Knit into the front and back

Slip 1 purl stitch to cable needle and hold in back, K2, P1 from cable needle

Slip 2 knit stitches to cable needle and hold in front, P1, K2 from cable needle

Slip 2 stitches to cable needle and hold in back, K2, K2 from cable needle

Slip 2 stitches to cable needle and hold in front, K2, K2 from cable needle

Slip 2 purl stitches to cable needle and hold in back, K2, P2 from cable needle

Slip 2 purl stitches to cable needle and hold in front, P2, P2 from cable needle

Slip 3 stitches to cable needle and hold in back, K3, K3 from cable needle

Slip 3 stitches to cable needle and hold in front, K3, K3 from cable needle

■ No stitch

[See pattern for specific directions.]

Abbreviations

CO	cast on		RS	right side
K	knit		WS	wrong side
P	purl		SSK	slip, slip, knit
PM	place marker		ST ST	stockinette stitch
K2TOG	knit two together		YO	yarn over
K3TOG	knit three together		K1F&B	knit into the front and back
KTBL	knit through back loop		WYIB	with yarn in back
P2TOG	purl two together		WYIF	with yarn in front
PSSO	pass slipped stitch over			

Standard Sock Sizes

The sizes given with each sock pattern indicate the number of inches or centimeters in circumference. Here, you can find standard lengths, corresponding to U.S. shoe sizes.

Standard Size Chart

S Women's Small   S Men's Small   S Child's Small: 2–4 yr old
M Women's Medium   M Men's Medium   M Child's Medium: 6–8 yr old
L Women's Large   L Men's Large   L Child's Large: 10–12 yr old

Women

SHOE SIZE	LENGTH IN INCHES	LENGTH IN CENTIMETERS
S 3	8	20.25
S 3.5	8.12	20.75
S 4	8.33	21.25
S 4.5	8.5	21.5
S 5	8.67	22
S 5.5	8.88	22.5
S 6	9	22.75
M 6.5	9.17	23.25
M 7	9.38	23.75
M 7.5	9.5	24
M 8	9.62	24.5
M 8.5	9.75	24.75
M 9	10	25.5
L 9.5	10.25	26
L 10	10.33	26.25
L 10.5	10.5	26.75
L 11	10.67	27
L 11.5	10.88	27.5
L 12	11	28
L 12.5	11.17	28.25

Men

SHOE SIZE	LENGTH IN INCHES	LENGTH IN CENTIMETERS
S 5	9	22.75
S 5.5	9.17	23.25
S 6	9.38	23.75
S 6.5	9.5	24
S 7	9.62	24.5
S 7.5	9.75	24.75
S 8	10	25.5
M 8.5	10.25	26
M 9	10.33	26.25
M 9.5	10.5	26.75
M 10	10.67	27
M 10.5	10.25	27.5
M 11	11	28
M 11.5	11.17	28.25
L 12	11.38	29
L 12.5	11.5	29.25
L 13	11.67	29.75
L 13.5	11.88	30.25
L 14	12	30.5
L 14.5	12.12	30.75
L 15	12.38	31.5

Standard Sock Sizes (cont'd)

Children

SHOE SIZE	LENGTH IN INCHES	LENGTH IN CENTIMETERS	SHOE SIZE	LENGTH IN INCHES	LENGTH IN CENTIMETERS
S 1	3.33	8.5	M 10	6.5	16.5
S 1.5	3.5	9	M 10.5	6.62	16.75
S 2	3.67	9.25	M 11	5 6.75	17.25
S 2.5	3.88	9.75	M 11.5	7	17.75
S 3	4	10	M 12	7.12	18
S 3.5	4.17	10.5	M 12.5	7.25	18.5
S 4	4.38	11	L 13	7.38	18.75
S 4.5	4.62	11.75	L 13.5	7.5	19
S 5	4.75	12	L 1	7.75	19.75
S 5.5	4.88	12.25	L 1.5	7.88	20
S 6	5.12	13	L 2	8.12	20.75
S 6.5	5.25	13.25	L 2.5	8.33	21.25
M 7	5.38	13.75	L 3	8.5	21.5
M 7.5	5.5	14	L 3.5	8.62	22
M 8	5.75	14.5	L 4	8.75	22.25
M 8.5	5.88	15	L 4.5	9	22.75
M 9	6.12	15.5	L 5	9.25	23.5
M 9.5	6.25	16			

Resources

Berroco
508-278-2527
www.berroco.com
Lang Jawoll

Cherry Tree Hill
802-525-331
www.cherryyarn.com
Superwash Merino Mini

Clover Needlecraft
800-233-1703
www.clover-usa.com
Chibi darning needles, locking stitch markers,
yarn bobbins

Eucalan
800-561-9731
www.eucalan.com
wool wash

Fiber Trends
debbie@fibertrends.com
www.fibertrends.com
sock blockers

Lorna's Laces
773-935-3803
www.lornaslaces.net
Shepherd Worsted

Louet North America
613-925-4502
www.louet.com
Louet Gems Merino Sport and Fine

OXO International
800-545-4411
www.oxo.com
salad spinners

Patternworks
800-438-5464
www.patternworks.com
huge yarn selection featured in beautiful
full-color catalogs and a great shop in
a picturesque New Hampshire town

Schaefer Yarn Company
607-532-9452
www.schaeferyarn.com
Schaefer Anne

Skacel Collection
800-255-1278
www.skacelknitting.com
Zitron Trekking XXL, Addi turbo needles

Unicorn Books and Crafts
800-289-9276
www.unicornbooks.com
Lana Grossa Meilenweit

WEBS
800-367-9327
www.yarn.com
known as America's Yarn Store: loads of yarn
and yarn-related supplies, including Valley
Yarns Superwash and Valley Yarns Kangaroo
Dyer Franklin

Westminster Fibers
800-445-9276
www.westminsterfibers.com
Regia Bamboo

The Sock Knitters

Although I designed all of the socks in this book, the socks shown in the photographs were knitted by the following talented women:

Emily's Socks (page 105), **H Sock**, and **Ragg Hiker**:
   Mary Alice Baker

Emily's Socks (cover): *Kathleen M. Case*

Belle Époque: *Kristen Gonsalves*

Coquette: *Karen Minott*

The Classic Sock and **Sugar Maple**: *Tamara Stone-Snyder*

Pitter Patter: *Katy Wight*

Acknowledgments

A lot of folks have helped me along this exhilarating and often bizarre journey, and this seems a good moment to name some names.

First, I thank God, who created me and gave me this mind and body to use; I am forever in awe and blessed.

Second, I give my appreciation to my husband, Gene, who never once looked at me and said, "I don't think that's such a good idea," but rather encouraged me to the point that I thought he might have lost his mind.

My father, too, deserves huge credit for always telling me I could be anything I wanted to be, as long as I was the best I could be. I know you sometimes wonder just where I am heading, Dad. Frankly, I am not always sure myself — but just trust me, it's a right path.

Next, a big and wordless but slightly weepy hug for my daughter, Megan, who daily stuns me; who's filled the dishwasher, walked dogs, fed chickens, and (so far) not once argued in spite of being in school full-time and working.

Kathy Elkins and Stephanie DiSantis each deserve a huge (as in gargantuan, monstrous, endless) "thank you" for saying I had darn well better write the book.

Special thanks to Lillian of New Fortune in Greenfield, Massachusetts, for the sushi and the unlimited green tea.

Most especially, I thank my group of intrepid sample knitters, who stood fast against my moderate insanity and in a couple of instances some pretty bizarrely written patterns: Mary Alice Baker, Kristen Gonsalves, Karen Minott, Rue Shanti, Tamara Stone-Snyder, and Katy Wight. Without you, and I mean this, guys, this book could not have made its deadlines. Your skill, feedback, support, great questions, and excellent suggestions have really been invaluable. I'd be pulling my hair out right this minute if it were not for you. Now we party!

INDEX

Page numbers in *italics* indicate photographs. Page numbers in **bold** indicate charts.

OTHER STOREY TITLES YOU WILL ENJOY

101 Designer One-Skein Wonders, edited by Judith Durant.
More patterns for every lonely skein in your
stash, from America's knitwear designers.
256 pages. Paper. ISBN 978-1-58017-688-0.

Knit Socks!, by Betsy Lee McCarthy.
From a best-selling series — 15 patterns for all levels of knitters,
paired with advice on knitting in the round on five needles.
144 pages. Die-cut hardcover. ISBN 978-1-58017-537-1.

The Knitting Answer Book, by Margaret Radcliffe.
Answers for every knitting quandry — an indispensable
addition to every knitter's project bag.
400 pages. Flexibind with cloth spine. ISBN 978-1-58017-599-9.

Kristin Knits, by Kristin Nicholas.
Hats, mittens, scarves, socks, and sweaters — inspired
designs for bringing your knitting alive with color.
208 pages. Hardcover with jacket. ISBN 978-1-58017-678-1.

Luxury Yarn One-Skein Wonders, edited by Judith Durant.
The one-skein concept meets luxury fibers, including alpaca,
silk, cashmere, and bamboo — fun, fast, and decadent!
272 pages. Paper. ISBN 978-1-60342-079-2.

One-Skein Wonders: 101 Yarn Shop Favorites,
edited by Judith Durant.
One hundred and one projects for all those single skeins
in your stash, collected from yarn shops across America.
240 pages. Paper. ISBN 978-1-58017-645-3.

These and other books from Storey Publishing are available
wherever quality books are sold or by calling 1-800-441-5700.
Visit us at *www.storey.com*.